Footprint Handbook
Valencia
& Cos

MARY-ANN

This is
Valencia
& Costa Blanca

The two Mediterranean autonomous communities of Valencia and Murcia are usually known collectively as El Levante. They may be next-door-neighbours, but they couldn't be more different. Green, fertile Valencia is famous for its orange groves and rice fields, yet much of Murcia is virtual desert. Valencia city is rapidly becoming one of the most dynamic and stylish cities on the Mediterranean, while Murcia's delightful little capital is much more low-key, but a great place to enjoy authentic Spanish traditions such as tapas out on flower-filled squares.

The two provinces do share the Mediterranean coastline, however, with all the attendant worship of sun, sea and sand. Don't give up hope of finding a secret cove: the closer you get to the Andalucía border, the more wild and remote the coastline becomes. Inland is a different story altogether. In Valencia, El Maestrat is a mountainous region of castle-topped towns. Beautiful historic towns like Xátiva, Gandía or Orihuela are a welcome respite from the giddy seaside resorts. Ancient traditions still linger, and these are best appreciated during the fiestas: Las Fallas is one of the biggest and best in Spain, but almost as well known are Alcoy's Battle of the Moors and the Christians, and Alicante's Las Hogueras. Murcia's interior is surprisingly green: the wild natural park of the Sierra de Espuña is still studded with traditional stone wells used until less than a century ago. There is also a string of lovely towns to explore, such as Lorca, with lavish baroque architecture, or monumental Caravaca de la Cruz.

Mary-Ann Gallgaher

Best of
Valencia
& Costa Blanca

top things to do and see

❶ Barrio del Carmen

This little corner of Valencia's lovely historic heart is packed full of bars, boutiques and terrace cafés, which has made it the epicentre of the city's nightlife. But it's also home to top cultural attractions like the Museum of Modern Art and the delightful museum-home of the painter Josep Benlliure, which comes complete with a secret garden. Page 15.

❷ Ciudad de Las Artes y Las Ciències

Santiago Calatrava's stunning City of Arts and Sciences is a vast cultural complex comprising a high-tech science museum, a planetarium in the shape of an eyeball, a performing arts centre which resembles billowing sails, and a vast aquarium (designed by Félix Candela) with Gaudiesque arched pavilions. Page 19.

❸ Benicàssim

Every July, this pretty whitewashed seaside resort explodes when the Festival Internacional de Benicàssim comes to town. Thanks to the fantastic line-up of top pop, rock and electronica artists, it has become one of the most popular music festivals in Europe, attracting more than 50,000 visitors annually. Page 32.

❹ Morella

This enchanting walled town crowns a peak in the remote, rugged region of El Maestrat. Morella's sturdy 15th-century walls encircle a beautifully preserved maze of narrow streets, squares and churches. In the surrounding hills, you can hike, swim in natural pools, hunt for the prized black truffles and explore sleepy villages. Page 37.

❺ Xàbia

The most westerly point of the Costa Blanca, Xàbia is tucked between two rugged headlands, which offer great opportunities for scuba diving and snorkelling. This vibrant resort is spread around a picturesque bay, and the surrounding coastline is dotted with scores of pebbly beaches and coves, many of which can only be accessed by boat or kayak. Page 45.

❻ Peñón de Ifach

Once a pirate hideaway and now a natural park, this massive outcrop of rock juts sheerly out of the sea in Calpe. You can climb to the spectacular viewing area at the top via a narrow panoramic path, or take one of the challenging climbing routes on the rock's seaward flanks. Page 45.

❾ Sierra de Espuña

This beautiful nature reserve high in the inland hills provides a wonderful, green oasis in the largely arid region of Murcia. Hike under the shade of the pine trees, go birdwatching, climbing or mountain-biking, or gaze at the other-worldly landscape of the badlands, the Barrancos de Gebas. Page 66.

❿ Calblanque

Calblanque is one of the last unspoilt stretches of Mediterranean coastline, its tranquil bays of golden sand backed by forests of pine and juniper, and rippling fossilised dunes. Protected as a nature reserve, it's home to rare and endangered plant and animal life, and is criss-crossed with walking paths. Page 71.

❼ Alicante

With its elegant palm-lined seafront and charming old quarter, Alicante is one of Spain's most genuine and enticing cities. Climb up to the medieval castle, high on a cliff, to enjoy fantastic views along the whole coast, and then join the locals in the *tapeo* – a tour of atmospheric tapas bars. Page 48.

❽ Murcia

A vibrant university town set in a lush valley, Murcia has a sprinkling of baroque buildings, including a lavish cathedral, plus plenty of charmingly offbeat sights and museums. Its most enduring attractions, however, are its delicious food, its appealing squares fringed with tapas bars and, above all, the friendliness of its people. Page 59.

L'umbracle, Ciudad de Las Artes y Las Cièncias, Valencia

València/
Valencia city

Historically, Valencia was never one of the big players in the Spanish tourist stakes, and it's hard to understand why. The old town is a delightfully compact little maze boasting palaces, markets, beaches, nightlife and restaurants. But Valencia's days as a wallflower are over. The city has become one of the coolest places on the Mediterranean, partly thanks to a revamp which saw the construction of Calatrava's futuristic Ciudad de las Artes y Las Ciències and the complete overhaul of the port.

But not everything has been successfully modernized. As a result of Spain's financial crisis, the building spree has come to a halt and the Valencia region has, unfortunately, become a poster child for rash public spending and cronyism thanks to the construction of a new airport in 2011 which only saw its first flight in 2015. However, the city does seem to be holding its own. The local festival of Las Fallas remains a classic – one of the biggest and wildest parties on the Spanish calendar – and Valencia continues to attract increasing numbers of visitors.

Essential València/Valencia city

Finding your feet

The narrow streets of the old city (about 4 km from the seafront) are best explored on foot and most of the main sights are clustered within easy walking distance of each other. Local buses will take you to places further afield like the City of Arts and Sciences (about 2.5 km west of the old town), the port and the Albufera. The metro system is aimed at commuters, but Line 4 (a tramline above ground) is handy for the beach at Malvarrosa. Taxis are easy to hail. The city-run bicycle rental network, **Valenbisi** (www.valenbisi.es), is available to short-term visitors as well as local residents; see website for full details. You can pick up and drop off bikes at one of the 275 stations around the city; purchase a pass at one of the automatic machines (approximately €13 per week, or a full year's subscription for €30).

Discount passes
Valencia Tourist Card This allows free entry and/or discounts at museums and attractions, as well as unlimited use of public transport (including the metro to the airport), plus discounts in shops and restaurants. It costs €15, €20 or €25 for one person and is valid for 24, 48 or 72 hours. You can buy it at tourist offices or online (with a 10% discount) at www.valenciatouristcard.com.

Museum Pass A one-day pass (*bono*) is available for municipally run museums, including the Museu d'Història de València. It costs €6, and is valid for three consecutive days.

> **Tip...**
> Seek out some of Valencia's offbeat attractions, such as the Casa-Museo Benlliure, which has a secret garden, and enjoy a stroll along the fabulous 9-km-long Túria Gardens.

When to go

Las Fallas, see page 18, in March is one of the best festivals in Spain, but book accommodation months in advance. Otherwise, early autumn is a lovely time when the rice fields turn gold.

Time required

Aim to spend at least a couple of days in Valencia, with one spent in the historic heart of the city, and another in the attractions of the City of Arts and Sciences. If you've got longer, head to the Albufera Lake and the wild beaches south of the city.

Weather València

January	February	March	April	May	June
14°C 5°C 24mm	16°C 6°C 30mm	18°C 6°C 21mm	19°C 8°C 36mm	21°C 11°C 33mm	25°C 15°C 15mm

July	August	September	October	November	December
28°C 16°C 6mm	28°C 17°C 18mm	26°C 15°C 42mm	22°C 11°C 36mm	18°C 8°C 42mm	15°C 6°C 30mm

The tree-lined Plaza de Ayuntamiento is filled with flower kiosks and overlooked by the 18th-century City Hall. It was completed in 1756 and given a twirly façade in 1915. This plaza is the focal point of the Fallas celebrations; not only does the fiesta kick off here, but this is also where the *fallas* are tossed onto the huge bonfire and burnt (see box, page 18).

Anyone arriving by local train will already have seen Valencia's delightful Modernista train station, the **Estación del Norte**, just west of the City Hall, with its whimsical mosaics and elaborate ticket booths. Next door is the **Plaza de Toros** (bull ring), which still sees plenty of action, particularly during the summer festival held in July.

Valencia is famous for its wealth of ornate baroque architecture, but the 18th-century **Palacio del Marqués de Dos Aguas** (to the north of the Plaza de Ayuntamiento) out-baroques the lot. Every inch of this giddy, marble-encrusted palace is carved in swirls and curlicues, and it is perhaps no surprise that the architect, Hipólito Rovira, died insane shortly after completing it. It's now the **Museo Nacional de Cerámica** ⓘ *C/Rinconada García Sanchís s/n, T963 516 392, Tue-Sat 1000-1400 and 1600-2000, Sun and holidays 1000-1400, €3/1.50, Sat afternoon and Sun free*, with a huge collection of ceramics gathered from all over Spain, particularly from Valencia itself. The top floor contains a typical tiled Valenciano kitchen. There are more tiles, along with paintings and sculpture, in the nearby baroque church of **San Juan de la Cruz**.

Colegio del Patriarca ⓘ *C/Nave 1, T963 514 176, 1100-1330, €7, admission by guided tour only, call in advance or book through website www.patriarcavalencia. es*, is a rare and elegant example of Renaissance architecture in baroque-crazy Valencia. The cloister, enclosed by ranks of slim marble columns, is particularly beautiful, and the small museum contains some outstanding artworks, including paintings by El Greco and Ribalta.

North of the Plaza de Ayuntamiento, Plaza de la Reina is an elegant square with terrace cafés and palm trees. Valencia's vast cathedral looms over one end, surmounted by the octagonal belltower, El Micalet (Miguelete), which has become the city's symbol.

Valencia's **cathedral** ⓘ *Mon-Sat 1000-1400 and 1700-1830, until 1730 in winter, Sun 1200-1630 until 1730 in winter €5/3.30, includes admission to museum and El Micalet belltower, www.catedraldevalencia.com*, was begun on the ruins of a mosque in the 13th century. Baroque craftsmen decided to tinker with it in the 18th century, and added the florid façade with thickly encrusted sculptural decoration and swooping lines. Just inside the main entrance, a doorway leads to **El Micalet**, which you can climb for staggering views across the whole city. The interior is light and elegant, and later embellishments have been stripped away to reveal the original Gothic features. The cathedral's greatest treasure is in the **Capilla del Santo Cáliz**, with an exquisite alabaster altarpiece which contains a jewel-studded chalice said to be that used at the Last Supper.

The **Museo de la Catedral** (for entry fee and opening times see above) has a collection of religious art, including a massive gold and silver Custodia, used for religious processions on the feast of Corpus Christi. The tour of the museum culminates in a small chapel containing two portraits of San Francisco de Borja by Goya (see Gandía, page 43). Both are dated 1788, but the second, showing the saint casting out sharp-toothed demons, prefigures Goya's later deeply unsettling *pinturas negras*.

Puerta de los Apóstoles leads out to the Plaza de la Virgen. The extravagantly sculpted doorway is the theatrical setting for the **Tribunal de las Aguas**, which

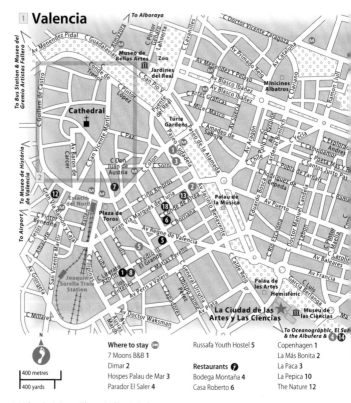

1 Valencia

Where to stay 🛏	Russafa Youth Hostel 5	Copenhagen 1
7 Moons B&B 1		La Más Bonita 2
Dimar 2	**Restaurants 🍴**	La Paca 3
Hospes Palau de Mar 3	Bodega Montaña 4	La Pepica 10
Parador El Saler 4	Casa Roberto 6	The Nature 12

takes place here every Thursday at 1230. Eight representatives from different parts of the city gather to discuss the city's water laws, just as they have since the custom was established by the Caliph of Córdoba in AD 960. The tribunal is held solely in Valenciano and fines are still meted out in the medieval currency. The ceremony is inscribed on UNESCO's intangible cultural heritage list.

Plaza de la Virgen

The graceful Plaza de la Virgen is the most beautiful of Valencia's squares, and is named after the **Basílica de Santa María de los Desamparados** ⓘ *0730-1400 and 1630-2100, free, museum €3, www.basilicadesamparados.org,* a sumptuous 17th-century church built to house a highly venerated statue of the Virgin of the Hopeless, the city's patron saint. The statue, which dates back to the early 1400s, is surrounded by a sea of candles and has pride of place in the vast, opulent interior. There is a small museum with a collection of religious painting and sculptures. Her feast day is celebrated on the second Sunday of May, when the whole square is covered with a carpet of flowers.

Palacio de la Generalitat ⓘ *T963 863 558, weekdays 0900-1400, free, book tours in advance,* just off the Plaza de la Virgen on Calle Caballeros, was built in 1510, an austere Gothic building with a graceful courtyard. The palace is now the seat of the Valencian government, but guided tours of the sumptuous Gothic interior can be arranged on weekdays. The Salón Dorado contains a spectacular *artesonado* ceiling, and the Salón de Cortes is richly decorated with azulejo tiles and frescoes.

A narrow lane snakes behind the Basílica to the **Plaza del Almoina**, where Roman baths, forum and bits of the Via Augusta have been excavated. The findings are displayed in the modern, high-tech **Museo Arqueológico de la Almoina** ⓘ *T962 084 173, mid-Mar to mid-Oct Tue-Sat 0930-1900, Sun 0930-1500, mid-Oct to mid-Mar 0930-1800, Sun 0930-1500, €2.* Just off the square is **Museo de la Ciudad** ⓘ *mid-Oct to mid-Mar Tue-Sat 0930-1900, mid-Mar to mid-Oct Tue-Sat 0930-1800, Sun and holidays all year 0930-1500, free,* set in the 19th-century Palacio del Marqués del Campo. The main galleries contain

➡ **Valencia maps**
1 Valencia, page 12
2 Valencia centre, page 16

Riff **18**

Bars & clubs 🎵
Beer **13**
La Casa Blanca **7**

MYA L'Umbracle
Terraza **14**
Ubik Café **8**

BACKGROUND

Valencia

Valencia's coastline had been settled by traders long before the Roman city of Valentia was founded here in 138 BC. It was a modest settlement compared to Saguntum up the coast, and it wasn't until the 11th century that it began to prosper. Under Abd al-Aziz ibn Abi Amir, it became one of the mightiest cities of Al-Andalus. Briefly conquered by El Cid in 1094, it finally fell to the armies of the Reconquista in 1238, who resettled the land with Catalan and Aragonese families.

The 15th century was Valencia's Golden Age, a time of prosperous economic growth, vast building projects and excellence in the arts. But the expulsion of the Moors in 1609 heralded financial disaster; at a stroke, the city lost almost 40% of its population. It wasn't until the 19th century that Valencia made a comeback, amassing its fortune with silk, agricultural produce and ceramics. It was briefly the headquarters of the Republican government during the Civil War and is now the seat of the Autonomous Community of Valencia with a population of 809,000.

minor artworks from the middle ages onwards, and a modern annexe holds an appealingly bizarre collection of archaeological and ethnographical curiosities. Almost opposite the museum is the **Cripta de San Vicente Mártir** ① *T963 941 417, Tue-Sat 0930-1400 and 1730-2000, Sun and holidays 0930-1400, audio-visual show Tue-Sat at 1000, 1130, 1300, 1800, 1900, Sun and holidays 1030, 1130, 1230, 1330, €2/1*, a Visigothic burial chapel which was probably part of an early cathedral. It's displayed in the basement of an ultra-modern building, and a high-tech audio-visual tour outlines the history of the chapel.

Plaza del Mercado and around

noisy and atmospheric; a great place to sample local food

Spanish markets are quite simply stunning, both architecturally and in terms of the breathtaking array of fresh produce on offer. Valencia isn't known as 'Spain's Orchard' for nothing.

The Modernista **market** ① *Mon-Thu 0800-1430, Fri 0800-2030, Sat 0800-1500*, is one of the prettiest in all of Spain, a vast concoction of wrought iron and stained glass surmounted with whimsical weather-vanes. The streets surrounding the market are packed with quirky, old-fashioned shops and the area is always buzzing. Get there early to catch it in full swing – breakfast at one of the counter bars is a must.

Facing the market is **La Lonja** ① *Mon 0930-1400, Tue-Sat 0930-1900, Sun 0930-1500, €2/1*, the former Silk Exchange, a spectacular World Heritage Site, which was built in the 15th century when Valencia was booming and is one of the finest examples of civic Gothic architecture in Europe. It's best visited on

Sunday mornings when the stamp and coin market gives the place a little of the commercial buzz which would have animated it 500 years ago. Upstairs, the offices of the Consulado del Mar are reached by a spiral staircase and contain a magnificent artesonado ceiling.

A low-key market spreads around this slightly dilapidated neighbourhood on most mornings. It's biggest on Sundays, when toothless old men offer puppies for a song in the narrow, run-down streets which splinter off from the **Plaza Redonda**.

Barrio del Carmen
bohemian area with great restaurants and nightlife

★Barrio del Carmen, usually simply known as El Carmen, is one of the hippest neighbourhoods in Valencia, stuffed with arty little cafés, shops, galleries, bars and restaurants; it's the best place in the city for an aimless wander. The little Plaza de Carmen, with a charming Gothic church topped with a winsome angel, is a good place to start.

Valencia's excellent **Instituto Valenciano de Arte Moderno (IVAM)** ⓘ *C/Guillem de Castro 118, www.ivam.es, T963 863 000, Tue-Sun 1000-1900, €2/1, free on Sun*, is housed in a vast, uncompromisingly modern building on the edge of El Carmen. The museum of modern art houses 19th-century artworks and changing displays of Valenciano crafts and exhibitions by local artists. The centrepiece of the permanent collection is an extensive array of sculpture by Julio González. Other highlights include ethereal seascapes by Joaquin Sorolla, some edgy blockish reliefs by Lucio Fontana, a delicate mobile by Alexander Calder, several boxy sculptures by Eduardo Chillida, and paintings by Antoni Tàpies. The museum holds excellent temporary exhibitions.

Not far from IVAM, you can step back in time at the **Casa-Museo José Benlliure** ⓘ *C/Blanquería 23, T962 911 662, mid-Mar to mid-Oct Tue-Sat 1000-1400 and 1500-1900, mid-Oct to mid-Mar 1000-1400 and 1500-1800, €2/1, included on 1-day Museum Pass (see page 10), free on Sun*, the former home of the famous 19th-century Valenciano painter, which has been filled with period furniture and fittings. The highlight is the magical little garden at the back. Filled with tiles, fountains and shady palms, it's a delightful and utterly unexpected oasis in the middle of the city. At the end of the garden is Benlliure's light-filled studio, which contains his magpie collection of ceramics, swords and artworks.

This section of the city is scattered with the remnants of the 14th-century walls and towers which once enclosed the old city of Valencia. **Torres de Cuart** are impressive, but the most spectacular are a few hundred metres downriver. **Torres de Serranos** ⓘ *Plaza de los Fueros, T963 919 070, mid-Mar to mid-Oct Tue-Sat 0930-1900, Sun and holidays 1000-1500, mid-Oct to mid-Mar 0930-1800, Sun and holidays 1000-1500, €2/1, included on 1-day municipal Museum Pass (see page 10), free on Sun*, two sturdy crenellated towers guarding a narrow gateway, are a popular symbol of the city and visitors can climb up for panoramic views.

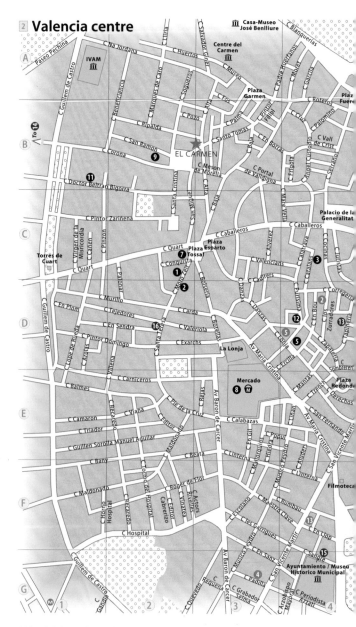

② Valencia centre

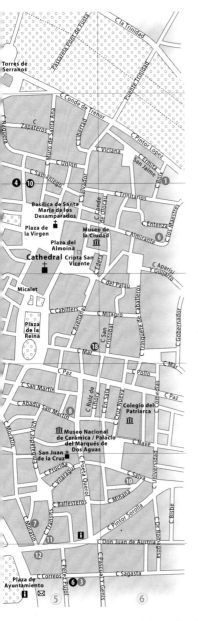

➡ **Valencia maps**
1 Valencia, page 12
2 **Valencia centre, page 16**

100 metres

100 yards

Where to stay 🏨

Ad Hoc **1** *B6*
Antigua Morellana **2** *D4*
Caro **6** *C6*
Florida **4** *G3*
Hôme International
 Youth Hostel **5** *D4*
Hostal Moratín **7** *F5*
Pensión París **10** *F6*
Pensión Universal **11** *F5*
Reina Victoria **12** *G5*
SH Inglés **8** *E5*
Sweet Continental **3** *G5*
Venecia **13** *F4*

Restaurants 🍴

Atmosphère **2** *D2*
Bar Pilar **1** *C2*
Bodeguilla del
 Gato **3** *C4*
Café de las Horas **4** *B5*
Café Lisboa **5** *D4*
Casa La Pepa **7** *C2*
La Central **8** *E3*
La Lluna **9** *B2*
Mesclat **11** *B1*
Seu-Xerea **10** *B5*
Tasca Ángel **12** *D4*
Vuelve Carolina **6** *G5*

Bars & clubs 🍸

Café del Duende **14** *B1*
La Siesta **13** *D4*
Mogambo **15** *G4*
Radio City **16** *D2*
Sol i Lluna **18** *D5*

Fun at the fiesta

Valencia's festival of Las Fallas is one of the fieriest and most important fiestas in Spain. It dates back to the Middle Ages, when carpenters used to light a bonfire in honour of Sant Josep, their patron saint. Gradually, effigies were thrown onto the fire, often depicting rival organizations.

Now, the vast creations made of papier-mâché, wood and wax take a year to build and are paraded through the streets from the 13-19 March. They can be of anything – cartoon characters, politicians, buxom ladies, animals – and each neighbourhood organization vies to create the best. They are accompanied by mini-versions, called *ninots*, and the winning *ninot* is the only one to escape the flames. Each day, firecrackers blast out over the Plaza de Ayuntamiento at 1400 (*La Mascletá*), bullfights are held in the afternoons, and the evenings culminate with a massive firework display. On the 18th, the Virgen de los Desemperados, patron saint of the city, is honoured with a spectacular offering of flowers. The fiesta culminates on the 19th, when the fallas are thrown into an enormous pyre, the *Cremá*. Prize-winning *fallas* are kept till last – but none escapes the flames.

You can see the prize-winning *ninots* and find out more about the history of the event at the engaging **Museo Fallero**, Plaza Monteolivete 4, T963 525 478, www.fallas.com, Monday-Saturday 0930-1900, Sunday and holidays 0930-1500, €2. To find out how the *fallas* are built, visit the **Museo del Gremio Artistas Falleros**, Avenida San José Artesano 17, T963 479 623, www.gremiodeartistasfalleros.com, Monday-Saturday 1000-1400 and 1600-1900, Sunday 1000-1330, €2.

Along the River Túria

great area to escape the city bustle, especially for children

River Túria was prone to flooding and has long since been diverted. The empty riverbed has been converted into one of Spain's largest and loveliest public gardens, which extend for 9 km.

Puente del Real crosses the Túria riverbed towards Valencia's **Museo de Bellas Artes** ⓘ *C/San Pío V s/n, T963 870 300, www.museobellasartesvalencia.gva.es, Mon 1100-1700, Tue-Sun 1000-1900, free*. While the museum has plenty of dull but worthy works by local artists, it also boasts a sizeable collection of treasures by El Greco, Ribera, Murillo, Van Dyck, Velázquez and Bosch, including the only self-portrait by Velázquez. Another highlight is the painstakingly rebuilt courtyard of the Ambassador Vich, an impressive 16th-century cloister built in the Italian style for the ambassador's elegantly remodelled Gothic mansion. Just beyond the Museo de Bellas Artes, the leafy **Jardines del Real** ⓘ *0600-2200, free*, are a good place for a picnic.

Carry on walking to the end of the riverbed and you will arrive at **Museu d'Història de València (Mhv)** ⓘ *C/Valencia s/n, T963 701 178, Apr-Sep Tue-Sat 0915-*

1400, 1630-2000, Sun and holidays 0915-1400, cost €2/1, Museum Pass €6, also valid.
One of the city's shiny contemporary museums, this presents 22 centuries of history with the latest 21st-century technology. Audio-visuals, computer simulations and even a time machine bring the past to life: you can see what the city looked like when it was founded, how the cathedral was built in the Middle Ages. It is a bit of a trek but well worth it, especially if you have kids in tow.

Kids will be even more impressed by the modern zoo, the **Bioparc** ⓘ *Av Pío Baraja s/n, T902 250 340, www.bioparcvalencia.es, open daily 1000-1800 or later (hours change weekly: check on the website), €23.80/18*, which has become – along with the City of Arts and Sciences – the city's biggest attraction. The animals are kept in surroundings which mimic, as far as possible, their natural habitats, with an emphasis on wide open spaces. Recently, the appearance of the zoo's first baby zebra has delighted the public.

La Ciudad de Las Artes y Las Ciències (The City of Arts and Sciences)
family-oriented attractions with spectacular modern architecture

★Valencia couldn't fail to see how new architecture had revitalized the fortunes of Barcelona up the coast, and the glossy City of Arts and Sciences was partly commissioned in order to raise the city's international profile. The gamble paid off: the futuristic complex designed by local celebrity architect Santiago Calatrava has been an overwhelming success since it was inaugurated in 1995. The complex contains, among other attractions, a superb science museum, the Museu de les Ciències; a planetarium, the Hemisfèric; and an immense aquarium, the Oceanogràfic. The Palau de les Arts, a billowing concert hall, has a full programme of cultural events.

Museu de les Ciències
Mon-Thu 1000-1800, Fri-Sun 1000-1900, daily 1000-2100 in summer, €8/6.20, temporary exhibitions cost extra.

The vast, white and glassy Museu de les Ciències looks like a hangar for spaceships, and the chirpy staff in turquoise uniforms add to the sense of a 23rd-century airport. It's a brilliant science museum, with excellent interactive exhibits and all kinds of gimmicks to teach kids – and everyone else – about everything from how the body works to what electricity is.

L'Hemisfèric
Mon-Thu 1100-200, Fri-Sun 1100-2100, €8.80/6.85.

Next door to the museum is the vast eyeball-shaped Hemisfèric, which is surrounded by a shallow lake, and contains a huge planetarium, with shows projected onto an enormous domed screen – book early, particularly at weekends.

Tip...
You can buy individual tickets to each of the attractions or a combined admission pass for 3 sights (valid over 2 or 3 days, €36.25/27.55 reductions).

L'Oceanogràfic
Weekdays 1000-1800, weekends 1000-2000, €27.90/21.

Housed in a series of beautifully sculpted pale pavilions, this is one of the biggest aquariums in Europe. The aquarium recreates the world's most important marine ecosystems and is home to 45,000 fish and marine mammals. The biggest attraction by far is the massive dolphinarium, with a school of 20 bottlenose dolphins, while the creepiest and most popular is the moving walkway through the vast shark tank.

Palau de les Arts
Av Autopista al Saler 1-7, T902 100 031, www.cac.es.

The final element of the complex is the stunning Palau de les Arts, which looks a bit like a ship in full sail. This is the city's principal opera house and concert hall, with a wide-ranging programme of music, dance and opera performances (see page 26).

Port and Playa Malvarrosa
the wide clean city beach offers a break from sightseeing

Valencia's port is the largest in Spain. As part of the preparations for the America's Cup, held here in 2007 and 2010, it was also endowed with a glossy marina, Spain's largest, which is now surrounded by fancy bars and restaurants.

Playa Malvarrosa is where everyone in Valencia comes to party during the summer months. It is the closest city beach, a long golden strand lined with bathing huts and excellent seafood eateries, and is a perfectly good place to sunbathe; however, the water suffers from pollution. At the end of the Playa de Malvarrosa is the low-key suburb of **Alboraya**, the birthplace of *horchata* (*orxata* in Valenciano), a refreshing drink made from tiger nuts.

Llac Albufera
a cycle ride from the city or a half-day trip

Llac Albufera sits about 10 km south of Valencia. The lake and surrounding area must have been beautiful once – it still is at dusk – but it's hard to block out the industrial buildings which surround it and even harder to ignore the contamination of the water by local factories. Despite the pollution, the area is still well known for its rice, used in the famous paella, and these marshy wetlands are also home to several species of water bird.

There's information on walking trails at the **park information office** ⓘ *Racó de l'Olla, T961 627 345, open 0900-1400*, near the attractive village of El Palmar.

Tourist information

Valencia tourist offices
Plaza de Ayuntamiento, T963 524 908, www.turisvalencia.es, Mon-Sat 0900-1900, Sun 1000-1400; Estación Joaquín Sorolla, C/San Vicente 171, T963 803 623, Mon-Fri 0900-1830; Airport (Arrivals), T961 530 229, Mon-Fri 0830-2030, Sat 0930-1730, Sun 0930-1430 (until 1730 in summer); also at C/Paz 48, T963 986 422, Mon-Fri 1000-1800, Sat 1000-2000 (this is the tourist office for the Comunidad de Valencia).

Where to stay

The choice of hotels has improved in the last few years, but chain hotels continue to predominate. The city offers a particularly good selection of holiday rental properties.

€€€€ Caro Hotel
C/Almirante 14, T963 059 000, www.carohotel.com.
Perhaps the most chic address in town, this exquisite, 19th-century mansion near the cathedral pairs minimalist contemporary design with a wealth of charming original details. The fabulous restaurant and bar are popular with the city's fashion pack.

€€€€ Hospes Palau de Mar
Av Navarro Reverter 14, T963 162 884, www.hospes.es.
One of the city's swankiest hotels, set in an exquisitely restored *palacete*, with lots of luxurious extras including a spa and pool. Online deals can drop it a couple of categories in the low season.

€€€€ Parador El Saler
Playa del Saler, T961 611 186, www.parador.es.
A modern parador overlooking sand dunes and surrounded by pine forest, with an 18-hole golf course, pool and restaurant.

€€€ Ad Hoc Monumental Hotel
C/Boix 4, T963 919 140, www.adhochoteles.com.
A chic little hotel in a converted 19th-century mansion. Exposed brickwork and beams are complemented with a mixture of modern and antique furnishings. The restaurant (expensive) serves Mediterranean fare with the emphasis on organic produce – and the lunchtime fixed menu is excellent value.

€€€ Hotel Dimar
C/Gran Vía Marqués del Túria 80, T963 154 012, www.hotel-dimar.com.
Ignore the unprepossessing exterior: inside you'll find stylish, modern rooms, with minimalist furnishings and a/c. Hotel amenities include a sauna, gym, and massage service, plus a café-restaurant. You can stroll along the Túria gardens to the historic centre in under 10 mins.

€€€ Reina Victoria
C/Barcas 6, T963 520 487, www.husa.es.
Reina Victoria's heyday has long past, but, if it's faded glamour you're looking for, this handsome turn-of-the-20th-century hotel has it in spades. Bland rooms are a disappointment, but the art deco salon is a treat.

€€€ SH Inglés
Marqués de Dos Aguas 6, T963 516 426, www.inglesboutique.com/en.

Set in a former palace overlooking the flamboyant ceramics museum. Rooms are comfortable but lack individuality given its palatial setting. Service is attentive and friendly and the excellent restaurant is a place to be seen.

€€ 7 Moons B&B
Av Navarro Reverter 13, T963 943 555, www.7moons.es.
Bright, airy rooms (with a choice of shared or private bathrooms) with stylish modern design in a fantastically central location: the best room has a private terrace. Buffet breakfasts.

€€ Antigua Morellana
C/en Bou 2, T963 915 773, www.hostalam.com/en.
A delightful *hostal* housed in an 18th-century house just a step from the Lonja and the Mercado Central. Clean, well-equipped rooms (all with bathrooms and TVs), plus a little sitting room. Location couldn't better for sights and nightlife. Prices often drop a category in low season. Recommended.

€€ Florida
C/Padilla 4, T963 511 284, www.hotelfloridavalencia.es.
A large, friendly *hostal* with simple, modern rooms, which prides itself on offering hotel facilities for guesthouse prices. Amenities include a/c, and some rooms have balconies.

€€ Sweet Continental
C/Correos 8, T963 535 282, http://sweethotelcontinental.com.
A reasonable modern hotel in a central location with good-sized rooms with all mod cons, including a/c. Lobby has a chic, boutique feel, but the rooms are more functional.

€€ Venecia
C/El Llop 5, T963 524 267, www.hotelvenecia.com.
A grand, turn-of-the-20th-century mansion overlooking the Plaza de Ayuntamiento, this offers immaculate a/c rooms, a range of services (including private parking and a buffet breakfast) and some of the most helpful staff in the city. Recommended.

€ Hôme International Youth Hostel
C/de la Lonja 4, T963 916 229, www.homeyouthhostel.com.
A colourful youth hostel with funky retro design in an elegant old building behind the Lonja, with accommodation in brightly painted dorms or a couple of twin rooms. They also have another branch, the **Home Backpackers Hostel**, www.homebackpackersvalencia.com, which offers cheap dorm accommodation in the trendy Carmen neighbourhood.

€ Hostal Moratín
C/Moratín 14, T963 521 220.
Friendly little *pensión*, offering pristine, basic rooms at low prices. Recommended but there is no a/c (fans are provided) so it can get hot in summer.

€ Pensión París
C/Salvá 12, T963 526 766, http://pensionparis.com.
Set in a charming century-old building, with basic but comfortable rooms, most with balconies, which come with a choice of private or shared bathrooms.

€ Pensión Universal
C/Barcas 5, 2º, T963 515 384, www.pensionuniversal.com.
A friendly, family-run *pensión* with good-value, spotless rooms in an excellent location just off the Plaza del Ayuntamiento.

€ Russafa Youth Hostel
C/Padre Perera 1, T963 289 460,
www.russafayouthhostel.com.
This colourful and friendly hostel offers
bargain beds in dorms or private rooms
in the trendy Ruzafa neighbourhood, a
stone's throw from the historic centre.

Restaurants

€€€ Ricard Camarena Restaurant
*C/Dr Sumsi 4, T963 355 418, www.ricard
camarena.com. Closed Sun and Mon.*
Chef Ricar Camarena has won countless
awards for his spectacular, highly
imaginative contemporary cuisine, and
you'll need to book well in advance
for a table. Choose between a 6-, 9- or
11-course set menu, or go à la carte, and
let your palate be dazzled. Prices are high
(€60-120 per head) but they also do an
excellent set lunch for €35.

€€€ Riff
*C/Comte d'Altea 18, T963 335 353,
www.restaurante-riff.com. Closed Sun
and Mon.*
A sleekly designed modern restaurant
serving excellent contemporary
Valenciano cuisine from Bernd Knöller.

€€€ Seu-Xerea
*C/Conde de Almodóvar 4, T963 924 000.
Closed Sun.*
A super-hip restaurant serving unusual
fusion dishes. Pick from a selection of
set menus, which include a tapas menu
(€35, plus €10 with wine pairing) and
an excellent *menú de degustación*
(tasting menu, €49, plus €15/20
with wine pairing).

€€ Casa Roberto
*C/Maestro Gozalbo 19, T963 951 361,
www.casaroberto.es. Closed Mon and
throughout Aug.*

> **Tip...**
> Ricard Camarena has got Valencia
> locked up when it comes to great
> eateries: his burgeoning empire
> includes his flagship restaurant, with
> a Michelin star, plus the fantastic bistro
> in the Mercat Central. As Valencia is
> the birthplace of paella, don't miss the
> chance to enjoy an authentic paella
> at one of the beachfront restaurants
> along the coast.

Pictures of famous bullfighters set the
scene in this traditional stalwart, a great
place to try an authentic paella.

€€ Copenhagen
*C/Literato Azorín 8, T963 289 928,
www.copenhagenvalencia.com.*
Sleek, Scandi-style decor and delicious
veggie cuisine make this a fantastic
option for lunch or dinner.

€€ La Pepica
*Paseo de Neptuno 6, T963 710 366,
www.lapepica.com. Closed Sun dinner.*
Large, lively, perennially popular seafood
restaurant overlooking the seafront that
has been going for more than a century.

€€ Vuelve Carolina
*C/Correos 8, T963 218 686, www.
vuelvecarolina.com. Closed Sun.*
Renowned chef Quique Dacosta is
behind this fashionable gastrobar,
which serves sophisticated tapas and
contemporary interpretations of classic
Valencian rice dishes.

€ Bar Pilar
C/Moro Zeit 13, T963 910 497.
A timeless old bar just off the Plaza del
Esparto, where you should eat mussels
(*clòtxines* in Valenciano, *mejillones* in
Castellano) and toss the shells in the
buckets under the table.

ON THE ROAD

Grain in Spain

Valencia is the birthplace of paella. Paella is not the unnaturally yellow dish advertised in five languages on laminated menus across the world, but an umbrella term for a vast array of rice-based dishes. The definitive paella is a chimera – most Spaniards claim they have the recipe, but it's never the same as anyone else's – but some things remain constant. The dish is flavoured with garlic and saffron, cooked in a large flat pan, and the heat is turned up just before completion to ensure a thin crust on the rice called the soccarat. Paella can be made with meat – traditionally it was made with rabbit or snails – or with seafood (*paella de mariscos*), or occasionally just with vegetables (*paella de verdura*).

€ Casa La Pepa
C/Conquista 8 bajo, T963 925 447.
A charming, old-fashioned tapas bar and restaurant decorated with bullfighting posters and old photos.

€ La Lluna
C/San Ramón 23, T963 922 146.
A sweet, colourfully tiled place in El Carmen which serves a good range of veggie and vegan dishes. The set lunch menu is a great deal at just €8.

€ La Paca
C/Rosario 30, T637 860 528.
A delightful, shabby-chic café-bar in the seafront Cabañal neighbourhood, where you can enjoy their famous meatballs, or sit out on the charming terrace with a beer and a tapa for just a €1.

€ Mesclat
C/Beltrán Bigorra 10, T963 065 852.
A trendy gourmet burger bar, where you can choose from around 20 different types of burger, including Black Angus beef, langoustine and veggie.

€ The Nature
Plaza de Vannes 7, T963 940 141.
A cheap and cheerful vegetarian canteen-style place which does a good veggie buffet lunch or dinner for €8; Asian-influenced and Mediterranean dishes include noodles with tofu, stir fries, vegan pizza and pasta dishes.

Tapas bars and cafés

Atmosphère
C/Moro Zeit 6, in the Institut Français, T963 153 095.
Lovely French croissants and delicious light meals are on offer at this delightful café in the French Institute, which also has a pretty terrace. They also offer a great set lunch for around €11.

Bodega Montaña
C/José Benlliure 69, T963 672 314.
This traditional, buzzy tavern opened its doors in 1836 and offers an excellent range of quality wines and tapas. Highly recommended.

Bodeguilla del Gato
C/Catalans 10.
T963 918 235. A brick-lined tapas bar decorated with bullfighting posters with good, old-fashioned tapas and *raciones*.

Café de las Horas
C/Conde de Almodóvar 1, T963 917 336, www.cafedelashoras.com.

Just off the Plaza de la Virgen, this is a relaxed little café, good for coffee and cocktails, with theatrical drapes to keep customers cosy.

Café Lisboa
Plaça Del Dr Colledo 9, T963 919 484.
A big, if slightly pricey, favourite in the old centre, this looks out over a pretty square and serves great sandwiches and salads as well as cocktails in the evenings.

La Central
Mercat Central, T963 911 314, www.centralbar.es.
A fashionable bar in the spectacularly revamped surroundings of the Mercat Central, this offers superb tapas designed by award-winning chef Ricard Camarena (see also his flagship restaurant, above).

La Más Bonita
C/Cádiz 16, T961 143 611.
A very pretty, blue-and-white painted café near the beach, this serves fresh, organic cuisine. Perfect for a lazy brunch.

Tasca Ángel
C/Purísima 1, T963 917 835.
Unchanged in decades, this miniature bar has bright lights and a steel counter. Ignore the unappealing decor and focus on the fantastic and very reasonably priced tapas, especially the famous fried sardines.

Bars and clubs

Valencia's nightlife is concentrated in different 'zones' around the city, but the best place to start is the long-standing hipster barrio of **El Carmen** in the heart of the old city, or in the **Ruzafa** district in the modern Eixample area, where there are scores of stylish restaurants, clubs and bars. In summer, everyone piles down to the big bars and clubs near the **Malvarrosa beach**.

Beer
C/Salamanca, 4, T963 741 431, www.cerveceriabeer.com.
This calls itself *'el museo de la cerveza'*, with a massive range of local, Spanish and imported beers. A lively, studenty hang-out with a popular summer terrace.

Café del Duende
C/Turia 62, T630 455 289, http://cafedeluduende.com.
Popular, flamenco-themed bar with live performances.

La Casa Blanca
Paseo de Ruzafa 10, T963 511 250.
Perhaps the best gin-and-tonics in town, and a great terrace for watching the world go by.

Mogambo Club
C/de la Sangre 9.
Very popular disco-bar with different DJs nightly.

MYA/Umbracle Terraza
Av del Saler 6.
This fancy *terraza* (summer club) has a spectacular setting in the Umbracle, part of the City of Arts and Sciences.

Radio City
C/Santa Teresa 19, T963 914 151, www.radiocityvalencia.com.
Live music, flamenco, poetry readings and much more at this Valencia classic.

Sol i Lluna
C/del Mar 29, T963 922 216.
A great, relaxed bar and restaurant in the Carme neigh bourhood with a spacious terrace for those hot summer nights and a good restaurant attached.

Ubik Café
C/Azorín 13, T963 741 255, http://ubikcafe.blogspot.com.es.

This charming bookshop and café is a relaxed spot for a quiet drink, and also hosts all kinds of activities, including jazz and flamenco concerts.

Entertainment

To find out what's on, pick up the Fri edition of the local paper *El Levante* which has a listings supplement, or get the free *Hello Valencia* magazine from the tourist office, also available online at www.hellovalencia.es. *Cartelera Turia* (€2) has the most extensive arts and cultural listings (in Spanish). The English-language freebie *24/7 Valencia* (available online at www.247valencia. com) is an excellent resource, particularly for nightlife.

Cinema
Films shown in their original language are listed as VO (*versión original*).
IVAC Filmoteca, *Plaza de Ayuntamiento 17*, *T963 539 300*, *http://ivac.gva.es/la-filmoteca*. Film seasons featuring cult classics, foreign films and special events.

Live music
Black Note, *Av Poly y Peyrolón 15*, *T963 933 663*, *www.blacknoteclub.com*. Live music nightly in El Carme – everything from jazz, blues and flamenco to rock, soul and funk.
Jimmy Glass, *C/Baja 28*, *www.jimmy glassjazz.net*. A dim, photo-lined jazz bar with fortnightly gigs.

Football
FC Valencia, *www.valenciacf.com*, are a big, popular football team, but it's not impossible to get tickets for a match in the Mestalla stadium.

Theatre and classical music
Palau de la Música, *Jardines del Túria*, *T963 375 020*, *www.palaudevalencia.com*. Huge glassy building overlooking the Túria for classical music, opera, ballet and occasionally pop and jazz.
Palau de les Arts, *Ciudad de las Artes y las Ciencias*, *T902 100 031*, *www.lesarts. com*. Calatrava's stunning concert hall looks like a futuristic galleon. Built to 'democratize' the arts and provide a dynamic mixture of classical and contemporary theatre, opera, dance and music.
Teatro Principal, *C/Barcas 15*, *T963 539 200*. Varied drama, musicals, opera, and ballet.

Festivals

Mid-Mar Las Fallas, Valencia's biggest festival – see box, page 18.
Jul Feria de Julia, with outdoor parades and concerts, a 'Battle of the Flowers' and bullfighting.

Shopping

Valencia is a great place for shopping. The old city throws up trendy, quirky fashion (Barri del Carme mainly) as well as the cool and contemporary. Around Plaza Redonda is the place to find timeless old-fashioned shops.

Abanicos Carbonell, *C/Castellón 21*, *T962 415 395*, *www.abanicoscarbonell.com*. This shop has been making exquisite handmade fans for almost a century.
FNAC, *C/Guillem de Castro 9*, *T963 539 000*. Books, CDs, city maps, with a good selection in English.
Las Añadas de España, *C/Játiva 3*, *T963 533 845*, *www.lasanadas.es*. An excellent wine merchant and deli.

Mercado Colón, *C/Jorge Juan 19, T963 371 101*. Beautifully renovated Modernista market, which is now full of fashionable shops, restaurants and tapas bars.
Momofuko, *C/Cádiz 67, T963 285 979, www.momofuko.com*. A wonderful spot in the Ruzafa area combining a fashion boutique with a café and workshop space.
Simple, *C/Cajeros 3, http://simple. com.es*. A charming shop featuring Spanish-made ceramics, baskets, lamps, woodwork and more, all beautifully displayed by the photographer owner.
Studio, *C/Purísima 8, T617 952 635*. Very stylish retro furniture and knick-knacks for the home, with a particularly good selection of lighting.

What to do

There's a swimming pool and sailing school at the **Real Club Náutico de Valencia** (Camino Canal 91, www.rcnv.es). The local tennis club, **Club Tenis Valencia** (C/Botánico Cavanilles 7, T963 690 558, www.clubdetenisvalencia.es). Golf fans can try out the **Campo de Golf El Saler** (Ctra Saler Km 18, T961 611 186), one of the finest Spain.

Transport

Air
Valencia Airport, T902 404 704, www. aena.es, is in Manises, 8 km west of the centre. There's a direct metro service into the city centre; trains depart roughly every hour (journey time 25 mins), Mon-Sat 0530-2230, Sun 0700-2100, €2.10 one way. There's also an airport bus (No 150) into the centre which departs every 25 mins (journey time 45 mins) from 0530-2200 (no service on Sun),

€1.45. Taxis are outside the departures hall and cost €20-23 to the city centre.
There are flights to destinations across Spain, including **Madrid**, **Ibiza**, **Barcelona**, **Málaga**, **Bilbao** and **Sevilla**.

Boat
Ferries for the **Balearics** leave from the port, T963 670 704, 4 km from the city centre; for details, **Acciona/ Trasmediterránea**, T902 454 645, www. trasmediterranea.com, and **Baleària**, T902 160 180, www.balearia.com.

Bus
The bus station, Av de Menéndez Pidal 3, T963 497 222, is on the edge of town; take bus No 8 or 79 for the city centre.
Services for **Barcelona** with **Alsa**, T902 422 242, www.alsa.es; **Madrid** with **Auto Res**, T915 517 200, and connections to most major Spanish and international cities.

Taxi
Radio Taxi Valencia, T963 703 333; **Radio Taxi Manises**, T961 521 155 (airport).

Train
The main terminus for long-distance and high-speed trains to Valencia is the modern **Joaquín Sorolla station**. It is located about 1 km (and linked by a shuttle bus) from the pretty Modernista train station, now mainly (although not exclusively) used for local and regional services.
To **Barcelona**, **Tarragona**, **Alicante** and **Murcia**, plus an hourly high-speed service to **Madrid** (between 0700 and 2000). Regional trains to **Castellón**, **Xàtiva**, **Gandia**, **Buñol**, **Requena** and **Utiel**.

Costa
del Azahar

A fertile plain covered with orange groves stretches north of Valencia, scarred by ugly ceramic factories puffing smoke. The long sandy beaches are popular with Spanish families, and particularly good around Benicàssim (famous for its excellent music festival). The main city, Castelló de la Plana, has little in the way of charm, but there are Roman ruins at Sagunto, and the remarkable papal city of Peñiscola piled on a rock.

El Puig

imposing hilltop monastery with a beautiful Gothic church

Heading northwards from Valencia, there's little to see for 18 km until the forbidding fortress-like monastery of El Puig comes into view.

Looming above the town, the **Real Monasterio de El Puig de Santa María** ① *T961 470 200, www.monasteriodelpuig.es.tl, visits Mon-Sat 1000 1100, 1200, 1600 1700, €4/3*, is still home to a community of monks. It's possible to visit the cloisters, salons and beautiful Gothic church as part of a guided visit. The eastern wing contains the **Museo de Artes Gráficas y La Imprenta** ① *Tue-Sat 1000-1400 and 1600-1800, Sun 1000-1400*, devoted to print and graphics, which counts the world's smallest book (look at it through a magnifying glass) among its treasures.

Sagunt/Sagunto

sleepy town with castle ruins and spectacular views

Sagunt (Sagunto in Castellano), north of El Puig, is a sleepy little town piled on to a hillside under a ruined castle. It's hard to imagine anything exciting ever happening here, but Sagunt made it into the history books in 218 BC when the Iberian villagers held out against Hannibal and his army for more than eight months, finally throwing themselves on to a burning pyre rather than capitulate.

The Romans rebuilt the city, and the most impressive surviving monument in modern Sagunt is the **Roman theatre** ① *C/Castillo s/n, T962 665 581, museum opens* *winter Tue-Sat 1000-1800, Sun and holidays 1000-1400, summer Tue-Sat 1000-2000, Sun 1000-1400, free.* It was completely and expensively restored, only for a judge to order the removal of the renovations after a case was brought by horrified locals who abhorred the concrete seating areas (local government has managed to stall the works, citing the expense). Nonetheless, it remains the focus of a famous cultural festival held here every summer. A dull archaeology museum is attached, with a smattering of ceramics discovered during local excavations.

The lofty **castle** ⓘ *T962 661 934, Mon-Sat 1000-2000, Sun and holidays 1000-1400, free*, is mostly in ruins, but part of it now contains an extensive collection of inscriptions, mostly Roman, but some dating back to pre-Roman times. A stretch of walls, squares and watchtowers still snakes impressively along the ridge for several kilometres, and offers stunning views across the old town and out to sea.

Listings Sagunt/Sagunto

Where to stay

There are few options in the old town, mostly on the main road. There are more options on the coast in Port de Sagunt, 5 km away.

€€ Hotel Les Arenals
C/Felisa Longas 1, Playa Almardá, T962 608 067, http://sweethotelarenals.com.
A modern, beachfront hotel with an outdoor pool and stylish rooms.

€ Azahar
Av País Valencia 8, T961 657 083.
A simple, central option on the edge of the old town, with friendly owners and air-conditioned rooms.

€ Carlos
Av País Valencia 43, T962 660 902.
A reliable budget option, located near the train station, offering basic but well-kept rooms.

Restaurants

€€ L'Armeler
Subida al Castillo 44, T962 664 382, www.larmeler.com.
This offers French and Mediterranean cuisine in a pretty, traditional townhouse.

€€ Racó de Paco
C/Joaquín Rodrigo 4, T962 650 987.
In the old town: tasty seafood and tapas in a wonderfully old-fashioned spot.

€ Mesón Casa Felipe
C/Castillo 21, T962 660 959.
This popular choice has a simple menu of cheap sandwiches and light meals.

The wild and beautiful region inland from Sagunt is dotted with tiny villages, wonderful natural swimming pools – and is blissfully free of crowds.

In **Vall d'Uixò**, 20 km north of Sagunt, boats wend along Europe's longest underground stream in the **Grutas de San José** ⓘ *Paraje San José s/n, T964 690 576, www.riosubterraneo.com*. It's a big tourist attraction, with all the attendant paraphernalia – snack kiosks, pool, playground.

Some 31 km northwest from Sagunt is the old walled town of **Segorbe**, surrounded by forested hills. There are several walking trails, including the GR10 in the nearby **Sierra Calderona**. It's a quiet, sleepy little place – except in early September, when bulls are chased through the streets for the wild festival of the **Entrada de Toros y Caballos**. The pretty old town is piled chaotically around the **Catedral de la Asunción** ⓘ *open 1100-1300*, originally built in the 12th century but subsequently given a showy baroque makeover. The second storey of the cloister contains the cathedral museum, with medieval altarpieces, paintings by Ribera and Ribalta, and some fine sculpture.

Deeper into the hills, about 35 km northwest of Segorbe is the little spa town of **Montanejos**, where you can take the waters at the **Fuente de los Baños** or lose yourself in the surrounding sierra which has good hiking and mountain-biking trails along spectacular gorges, many with beautiful natural swimming pools.

Listings Inland from Sagunt

Where to stay

€€ Hospedería El Palén
Segorbe, T964 710 740, www.elpalen.com.
A central and affordable hotel, set in an old beamed townhouse with a good restaurant (**€€**).

€€ María de Luna
Av Comunidad Valenciana 2, Segorbe, T964 711 313, www.hotelmariadeluna.es.
Modern and functional but the restaurant (**€€**) is recommended by locals, and serves delicious traditional cuisine.

€€ Rosaleda de Mijares
Ctra Tales 28, Monanejos, T964 131 079.
Next to the spa, this modern hotel is located right next to the natural swimming pools on the river.

€€ La Gruta
Passeig de les Grutes, La Vall d'Uixò, T964 660 008.
This romantic restaurant enjoys an unusual setting in one of the caves, and offers excellent modern Spanish cuisine.

€€-€ Xauen
Av Fuente Banos 26, T964 131 151, www.hotelxauen.com.
Reliable, modern option with a spa in Montanejos.

Transport

Segorbe is on the main train line from **Valencia** to **Zaragoza**, with several daily train connections.

Castelló is a modern provincial capital, with little in the way of sights or monuments but some decent beaches spread out around the port (called the 'Grao'). What remains of the old town (most of it was blasted to smithereens during the Civil War) is set back about 5 km from the Grao and the beaches, but there are shuttle buses from the Plaza Borrull. The few sights, and all the shops and services, are all in the old town, but there are restaurants and tapas bars by the port. Unfortunately, the city has become a byword for profligacy thanks to its huge white elephant of an airport, constructed at vast expense, and overseen by a €300,000 statue of the politician who commissioned it (now in jail for tax fraud). Completed in 2011, the airport will receive its first flight in late 2015.

Museo de Belles Artes ① *Av Hermanos Bou 28, T964 727 500, Tue-Sat 1000-2000, Sun and holidays 1000-1400, free*, is set in an 18th-century mansion, one of the few buildings to have survived the Civil War in Castellón, and contains works by Ribera, Ribalta, Sorolla and Benlliure. There's a small archaeological section, but it's best known for its extensive collection of ceramics from the 16th to the 19th centuries, and for the 10 paintings from the workshop of Zurbarán which are on loan from a local convent.

Espai de'Art Contemporani de Castelló (EACC) ① *C/Prim s/n, T964 723 540, www.eacc.es, Tue-Sun 1000-1400, 1600-2000, guided visits Fri 1900, free*, is a slick contemporary art museum, with a changing programme of temporary exhibitions featuring both established and rising new artists.

Listings Castelló de la Plana/Castellón de la Plana

Where to stay

Virtually all Castellón's hotels are modern and geared towards business travellers. This can mean good weekend discounts.

€€€ Tryp Castellón Center
Ronda Mijares 86, T964 342 777, www.hotelcastelloncenter.com.
Huge, white, modern chain hotel with a gym, pool and restaurant. Weekend deals can bring the prices down by up to 50%.

€€ Doña Lola
C/Lucena 3, T964 214 011.
Modern and comfortable; superior rooms come with kitchenettes.

Restaurants

€€€ Arropes
C/Benárabe, T964 237 658.
Delicious local rice dishes and seafood, and excellent service.

€€ Mediterraneo
Paseo de Buenavista 46, T964 284 609.
Tasty seafood from the nearby fish market, served up close to the seafront.

€€ Tasca del Puerto
Av del Puerto 13, T964 236 018.
A popular local restaurant by the port serving good rice dishes, seafood and home-made desserts.

€ Tapa Trece
C/Crevillente 7, T622 595 092.
Bright, modern tapas bar, offering great-value dishes which run the gamut from Spanish classics to more unusual fare.

€ Tertulia del Mar
Av del Mar 25, T964 229 100.
Great tapas, salads, sandwiches and rice dishes and a convivial atmosphere.

Tapas bars and cafés
There are dozens of good cafés and tapas bars around the Plaza Santa Clara (next to the Plaza Mayor), where all of Castellón seems to turn out for the evening *paseo* and for the summer concerts.

Bars and clubs

Castellón's students ensure that the nightlife is better than many towns of its size. The biggest clubs are on the outskirts of the city. The port area is liveliest in summer.

Transport

The combined bus and train stations are located on the edge of the town, with frequent connections to **Barcelona**, **Valencia**, **Madrid** and most major Spanish cities. It's about a 15-min walk to the town centre, and there's a local bus from outside the arrivals hall of the train station.

Benicàssim/Benicasim and around
popular seaside resort, host to an international rock festival

★Benicàssim is a family seaside resort, famous for the massive outdoor music festival held each year in July (www.fiberfib.com). The little village has been almost completely swallowed up by apartment blocks and restaurants, and there's nothing much to do but catch some rays.

Before the tourist boom, Benicàssim was known for the production of a sweet white wine, which can be tasted at the **Bodegas Carmelitano** ⓘ *Av Castellón s/n, T964 300 849, daily 0900-1330 and 1530-1900, €3, includes tasting.*

The seaside resort of **Oropesa**, a couple of kilometres north of Benicàssim, is not as chi chi as its neighbour and offers equally good beaches and cheaper accommodation. Lost in wooded hills a few kilometres inland from Benicàssim is the tranquil Carmelite monastery of the **Desierto de las Palmas** ⓘ *T964 300 950, www.desiertodelaspalmas.com, church 1000-1300 and 1600-1900 (until 2000 in Jul and Aug); museum open Sun 1200-1400.* Established three centuries ago as a place of retreat it still hosts workshops and meditation weekends. The church is open for visits and services, and there's an interesting museum of paintings and religious objects.

The region inland from Oropesa has been designated a **nature reserve**, also called the **Desierto de las Palmas**, and is criss-crossed with walking trails and picnic spots. There's a park information office at **La Bartola** ⓘ *Ctra del Desierto Km 8, T964 760 727.* You'll need your own transport, or else take a taxi (about €20).

Where to stay

Accommodation is surprisingly expensive in Benicàssim, and many places require half-board during Jul and Aug.

€€ Casa Arizo
C/Ramón y Cajal 50, Oropesa, T964 313 887.
A charming, family-run hotel in a beautiful century-old town house, with a handful of rooms which combine original Modernista details with contemporary furnishings. Recommended.

€€ Garamar
In town, near to the train station and beach.
Its sister hotel **€ Garamar II** is nearby. Both are basic.

€€ Hotel Bersoca
Av Jaume 217, T964 301 258, www.hotelbersoca.com.
A friendly, family-run hotel a block from the Els Terrers beach, with simple, comfortable rooms (all with balconies) plus an outdoor pool and a decent restaurant.

€€ Hotel Bosque Mar
C/Santo Tomás 73, Benicàssim, T964 046 153.
Simple, stylish rooms decorated with an arty touch in the historic town centre, about a 10-min walk to the beach.

€€ Hotel Bulevard
Av Castellon 2, Benicàssim, T964 390 226, www.bulevardhotel.com.
A good moderate option, with a small pool and modern, functional rooms.

Camping
There are several campgrounds all along the beachfront.

€ Bonterra Park
Av de Barcelona 47, T964 300 007, www.bonterrapark.com.
Large and well equipped, also rents out wooden bungalows.

Restaurants

There are lots of places along the seafront.

€ El Charquito
C/Santo Tomás 3.
Popular, traditional tapas bar with a summer terrace, serving local favourites at great prices.

€ La Llar
T964 305 559, www.lallar restaurante.com.
Fantastic paellas in a traditional setting.

Festivals

Jul **Benicàssim music festival**, http://fiberfib.com.

Transport

Benicàssim is on the train line between **Barcelona** and **Valencia**, with frequent connections to towns along the coast.

Peníscola

Peníscola is best seen from a distance. A tight mass of whitewashed houses piled on a rocky promontory and topped with a castle, it looks like a movie set – and movie buffs might recognize it from the film *El Cid*. Close up, the spell is quickly broken: the pretty cobbled lanes are gorged with coachloads of day-trippers, and the little whitewashed houses have been converted into brash cafés and souvenir shops. Still, as tourist towns go, Peníscola is as pretty as any on the Valencian coast. There's a **tourist office** ① *Paseo Marítimo, T964 480 208.*

Perched high above the tiled rooftops is the town's landmark, the 14th-century **Templar fortress** ① *T964 480 021, www.peniscola.es, summer 0930-2130, winter 1030-1730, €3.50/2.50,* which was later converted into a residence for pope Benedict XIII. During the Great Schism, the Church was split between Pope Urban VI in Rome and the rival Pope Clemente VII in Avignon. Benedict XIII succeeded Clut and it was during his reign that the Schism was resolved in favour of Rome and he found himself out of a job. He retired to Peníscola to create a third Papal City, but his successors failed to maintain it after his death. The castle is now a history and art museum, with a rather dull collection, but fabulous views.

The narrow isthmus which reaches out to Peníscola is lined with thoughtless modern development, but the beaches are long and sandy (if jam-packed in high season). The town still has a small fishing fleet, and the return of the brightly painted boats (around 1630) to the harbour is a beautiful sight.

Benicarló

The next coastal resort along from Peníscola is Benicarló, where the ranks of apartment blocks haven't quite wiped out the character of this former fishing village. The fishing fleet now sits alongside glossy yachts in the marina, and there's a pretty baroque church with a blue-tiled dome in the old town. The beach is small and popular with Spanish families, and the local speciality is artichokes – so prized that they have even been given their own *denominación de origen*, just like wines.

Vinaròs

A few kilometres further north from Benicarló is another fishing village-cum-seaside resort, Vinaròs. It's small and low-key, with the usual rash of concrete development along the beaches, but the port is still a hive of activity. The *langostinos* are famous throughout Spain, and the day's catch is auctioned off early each morning. Try them at one of the fancy seafood restaurants. There's a **tourist office** ① *Passeig de Colom, T964 453 334.*

Where to stay

There are plenty of options to stay in Peníscola, but book well in advance in Jul or Aug when prices jump.

€€€ Parador de Benicarló
Av Papa Luna 3, Benicarló, T964 470 100, www.parador.es.
The best place to stay in Benicarló is this modern option, with an excellent restaurant and pool.

€€€-€€ Hostería del Mar
Av Papa Luna 18, Peníscola, T964 480 600, www.hosteriadelmar.net.
One of the dozens of big hotels along the isthmus. Comfortable and old-fashioned, with a pool, restaurant and medieval-style banquets.

€€ Hotel Maryntón
Paseo Marítimo 5, Benicarló, T964 465 030, www.hotelmarynton.com.
Inexpensive studios and apartments right by the beach.

€€ Hotel Roca
Av San Roque, Vinaròs, T964 401 312, www.hotelroca.com.
Modern, excellent value, with pool and tennis. Just 250 m from the beach, and great for families.

€€ Mare Nostrum
Av Primo de Rivera 13, Peníscola, T964 481 626, www.hotelmarenostrum.net.
A simple, old-fashioned choice right on the seafront; the prettiest rooms have balconies overlooking the beach or port. Recommended.

€€ Pensión Chiki
C/Mayor 3, Peníscola, T964 480 284, www.restaurantechiki.com.
Cosy, traditionally furnished rooms in the old town, set above a great restaurant serving delicious traditional dishes.

€ Hostal Belmonte II
C/Pío XII 3, Benicarló, T964 471 239.
Sweet little family-run option in the old town.

€ Hostal Simo
C/Porteta 5, T964 480 620, Peníscola, www.restaurantesimo.es.
Good budget choice, with pretty rooms overlooking the water and a good restaurant.

€ Hotel Residence Sol
Avda Magallanes 103, Benicarló, T964 471 349, http://hotel-sol.com.
A friendly, family-run hotel, with a great pool and simple, inexpensive rooms.

Camping

€ Camping El Edén
C/Madrid s/n, Peníscola, T964 480 444, www.camping-eden.com.
One of several campsites, large and well equipped with a pool, café and supermarket, located about 2 km from the old town.

Restaurants

There's a daily market in Vinaròs for picnic supplies.

€€€ El Faro de Vinaròs
Puerto de Vinaròs s/n, Vinaròs, T964 456 362.
A refined seafood restaurant set in the old lighthouse, with a terrace offering views over the port. It offers a great value set menu for around €18.

€€€ El Langostino de Oro
C/San Francisco 3, Vinaròs, T964 451 204.
Classic seafood dishes. Mid-range
options too.

€€€ Parador de Benicarló
See Where to stay.
This parador has one of the best
restaurants in town.

€€ Casa Jaime
Av Papa Luna 5, Peníscola, T964 480 030.
Serves delicious fresh seafood on
the terrace.

€€ El Cortijo
*Av Méndez Núñez 85, Benicarló,
T964 470 075.*
Great, beautifully fresh seafood and what
many consider to be the best paella in
the area.

€€ El Peñón
*C/Santos Martires 22, Peníscola,
T964 480 716.*
Reliable, traditional restaurant which
does a cheap *menú del día* for under
€10. It also has inexpensive rooms.

Transport

Bus
There are shuttle buses from Vinàros
and Benicarló every 30 mins with **Autos
Mediteráneo**, T964 220 054, or you
could call a taxi (T964 460 506). There
are buses directly to the town centre
from **Barcelona** and **Zaragoza** with
HIFE, T902 119 814, www.hife.es, or from
Madrid with **Auto-Res**, T91 272 28 32,
www.avanzabus.com.

Train
The train station, with connections
along the coast between **Barcelona**,
Valencia and **Alicante**, is set back 7 km
at Benicarló.

Inland
Valencia

From the top of the province to the bottom there are some beautiful places to visit. To the north of Valencia is the historic and wild region of El Maestrat where hiking and other activities can be enjoyed. To the west are vineyards where bogedas can be visited. And then there are the mountainous villages belying their position just behind the often hectic action on the Costa Blanca.

El Maestrat/El Maestrazgo
mountainous region dotted with ancient pueblos; ideal for trekking.

Behind the Costa del Azahar is the wild and mountainous El Maestrat – a region of castle-topped villages which date back to the time of the Templars – a world away from the coastal fleshpots. There are excellent opportunities for hiking and adventure sports in the ravines and forests, but the region is difficult to explore without your own transport. The walled town of Morella is the only place which is well set up for tourists.

★Morella
Morella, surrounded by forested hills and surmounted with a lofty castle, is a heart-stopping sight. Hemmed in behind fortified walls bristling with towers, it's a beautiful old town of steep, cobbled streets and the cool mountain air makes it a popular weekend destination in summer.

Morella's main street, the Calle Blasco de Alagón, is lined with cafés and craft shops, and winds up steeply towards the lofty castle. Entrance is through the **Convento de Sant Francesc**, built in the 13th century and now used for temporary exhibitions. The main church contains fragments of Romanesque capitals and archways in the shallow chapels, and there's a pretty overgrown cloister gently tumbling into ruins. It's a long, hot climb up to the main square of the ruined castle, but the views are spectacular, sweeping across the hills and forests and looking out over a Gothic aqueduct below. East of the Convento de Sant Francesc is Morella's grandest church, the Gothic **Santa María la Mayor** ⓘ *Plaza Arciprestal, 1100-1400 and 1600-1800, free*, topped with a huge dome covered with deep blue tiles. It contains a beautiful 15th-century choir, and a gigantic baroque organ which features in the **Festival of Early Music** held in August. There's a small museum of religious art with a serene Madonna by Sassoferato.

One of the towers which stud the famous city walls has been turned into an interesting prehistoric museum, the **Museo Tiempo de Dinosaurios** ⓘ *1100-1400 and 1600-1800, until 1900 in summer, €2/1.50*, with bones, fossils and models of the Maestrat's ancient inhabitants.

The former **Iglesia de San Nicolás** is home to a delightful **museum** ⓘ *C/San Nicolás s/n, 1100-1400 and 1600-1800, until 1900 in summer, €2/1.50*, devoted to Morella's famous festival, the **Sexenni**, which is held every six years (the next one is in 2018). It began as a festival of thanksgiving to the Virgen de Vallivana, who saved the town from the plague in 1672. It's a wild nine-day affair, with parades, folk-dancing, a pilgrimage to the sanctuary where the image of the Virgin is kept, and mad confetti battles in the streets. Each street makes incredibly elaborate decorations from crêpe paper – recent versions have included a copy of Picasso's *Guernica* – and there's a prize for the best one.

Around Morella

Some 10 km west of Morella is **Forcall**, a modest village on the banks of the river, which is famous for its crafts and fine cuisine. Just beyond it is pretty whitewashed **Todolella** with a medieval bridge and a boxy castle, which is well known for its blood-curdling traditional dance, the **Danza Guerrera**, which you can see at the summer festival in August.

South of Morella, **Catí** has a twisting medieval core dotted with fine palaces, including the 15th-century Ajuntament. The landscape gets more rugged and mountainous as you head west towards the villages of the Alt Maestrat. Some, like tiny **Benassal**, are picturesque spa towns, and others, like striking **Vilafranca del Cid**, recall the legendary exploits of El Cid.

Northern Maestrat

The northern Maestrat is wilder and more mountainous than the south, and towns and villages are clamped to sudden rocky outcrops. This region is known as **Els Ports**, referring to the mountain passes, and some villages are uninhabited in winter. To explore it, you'll need your own car and probably your own provisions as there are very few places to stay or eat, although you can usually find rooms above a bar. The **Tinença de Benifassà (Setena de Benifassà in Valenciano)** is the collective name for a group of small villages that once belonged to the abbey of Benifassà, which sits on a tranquil hillside near **Bellestar**. From here, the road wriggles northwards towards tiny **Fredes**, with just two streets and a Romanesque church, and south to **La Pobla de Benifassà**, the largest of the villages in these parts, with sturdy stone houses still bearing the old wooden balconies typical of the region. **Embalse de Ulldecona** is a popular summer picnicking spot, and the forests and ravines offer endless scope for walks and bike rides.

Sanctuaries of El Maestrat

El Maestrat is scattered with sanctuaries which still draw in pilgrims from across Spain. Perhaps the most extraordinary is the lofty **Santuario de la Virgen de la Balma**, about 15 km north of Forcall, which is thickly hung with dolls' clothes and all kinds of other mementoes which have been left here in thanks for the Virgin's intercession. From here, the road squiggles madly towards Mirambel and Teruel in the Aragonese Maestrazgo.

There are more sanctuaries in the small towns which line the N232 between Morella and Vinarós including one at **Vallivana**, where the image of the Virgin responsible for saving Morella's inhabitants from the plague (see above) is kept. Perhaps the most famous of all is the **Santuari de La Mare de Déu de la Font de la Salut**, near the ceramic-producing village of Traiguera. Celebrated visitors to this 15th-century church, hospital and palace have included Cervantes and several Spanish monarchs. Southwest of Traiguera, **Sant Mateu** was once the capital of the region, and retains vestiges of its medieval grandeur.

Listings El Maestrat/El Maestrazgo

Tourist information

Tourist office
Plaza San Miguel, Morella, T964 173 032, www.morellaturistica.com.
Has leaflets showing the well-marked network of walking paths around the town and details of activities from pot-holing to mountain biking.

Where to stay

Tourist information offices have lists of *casas rurales* in the region. There is usually at least 1 bar in the villages of the Maestrat, some of which will rent rooms.

€€€-€€ Palau dels Osset
Plaza Major 16, Forcall, T964 171 180, www.palaudelsosset.com.
Set in a beautifully restored 16th-century palace, this also boasts an excellent restaurant. Recommended.

€€ Hotel Cardenal Ram
Cuesta Suñer 1, Morella, T964 160 046.
This beautifully converted 16th-century palace has rooms that are decorated with heavy wooden antiques and brightly coloured, locally made textiles. Highly recommended.

€€ Molí l'Abad
Ctra Pobla de Benifassá Km 7, La Pobla de Benifassá, T977 713 418, www.molilabad.com.
Set in a converted mill by the river, this is a large, yet tranquil, complex with a camping area, bungalows, and apartments. Pool, tennis courts and restaurant make it a popular option with families.

€ Aguilar
Av 3er centenario 1, Forcall, T964 171 106.
A simple hostal and restaurant, with inexpensive traditional local food.

€ Fonda Moreno
C/San Nicolás 12, Morella, T964 160 105.
A great budget choice, with simple, pristine rooms in the historic centre, and a generous breakfast. Great restaurant, too.

€ Hostal La Muralla
C/Muralla 12, Morella, T964 160 243.
Spotless, central, and friendly, although rooms lack charm.

Restaurants

Traditional, mountain food, particularly grilled meats (*carnes a la brasa*) predominates in the restaurants in El Maestrat.

€€€ Hotel Cardenal Ram
Morella, see Where to stay.
Very good.

€€€ Palau dels Osset
Forcall, see Where to stay.
A wonderful treat.

€€ Casa Roque
Cuesta San Juan 1, Morella, T964 160 336.
A cosy, traditional establishment in an old stone house, which specializes in truffles (a celebrated local delicacy) and offer several good value set menus, including a set dinner for €15.

€€ Mesón de la Vila
Plaza Mayor, Forcall, T964 171 125.
A charming spot, serving local dishes, which does a good-value *menú del día* for €15.

€€ Mesón del Pastor
Cuesta Jovani 7, Morella, T964 160 249.
Here, they serve tasty local specialities in the mid-range price category, including *croquetas morellanas*.

€€ Vinatea
C/Blasco Alagón, T964 160 744.
Has tables on Morella's porticoed main street, good for traditional cuisine and great tapas. The set lunch is a very reasonable €15.

What to do

You can walk to the ancient settlement of **Morella La Vella**, 6 km from Morella, where cave paintings have been discovered. **Aula Muntanya**, *Plaza San Miguel 3, Morella, T964 173 117, aulamuntanya@ morella.net.* Offers a range of adventure sports, from climbing and cyling to archery and botanical tours.

Transport

There are buses with **Autos Mediterráneo** (T964 240 778, www.autosmediterraneo. com), from **Castellón** (2 daily Mon-Sat, 2 hrs 15 mins) and **Vinarós** (2 daily Mon-Fri) for **Morella** (about €8 for a return ticket), but the times are not usually convenient for a day trip.

Sant Mateu and **Vallivana** are on the bus routes from the coast to **Morella** but there's no public transport to smaller villages.

West of Valencia
Bus
There are buses with **Monbus**, T902 292 900, www.monbus.es, between **Requena**, **Utiel** and **Valencia**.

Train
Requena and **Utiel** are on the regional train line from **Valencia** with connections to **Madrid**, **Cuenca**, **Ciudad Real** and **Albacete**. High-speed **AVE** trains stop at the Requena–Utiel station, located 5.5 km from Requena.

ON THE ROAD

Seeing red

No one really knows how La Tomatina started – stories range from a food fight at a wedding which got out of hand, to a tomato attack on a bad musician – but it's been going since the 1940s. Now it's one of the best-known festivals in Spain, attracting huge crowds every year. In fact, numbers have grown so much in recent years that Buñol's city council have introduced an admission charge and a limit on the number of participants. You can buy your admission tickets (which can include a bus trip from Madrid or Barcelona) in advance at http://latomatina.info. The event is now followed by the **Tomatina Sound Festival**, a music festival featuring big Spanish and international acts.

On the last Wednesday of August, everyone converges on the main square just before 1100 and starts yelling 'to-ma-tes, to-ma-tes', clapping and stamping their feet. Finally, an ear-splitting blast signals the arrival of trucks bearing thousands of tons of tomatoes. For a second or two, the crowd looks sheepish but suddenly a bacchanalian frenzy takes hold and all hell breaks loose. Within minutes, the ground is a slithering mess and everyone is red from head to toe, clothes hanging off them in rags. At the height of the frenzy, the siren sounds again and, miraculously, everyone obediently downs tomatoes. The fire brigade hose down the buildings and the grateful, panting participants. The canny ones have packed clean clothes and stashed them somewhere safe, but there's always the odd tourist who has to head back on the train soaked in tomato juice.

West of Valencia

low-key towns and a world-famous tomato festival.

West of Valencia are the wine towns of Requena and Utiel, modest little places which are probably only worth visiting if you are on your way to Aragón or Madrid. Buñol is the setting for La Tomatina, an ecstatic battle with thousands of tons of squashed tomatoes.

Buñol

Every year, thousands descend on Buñol for the world's biggest food fight, **La Tomatina** (see box, above). The other 364 days of the year, it remains a tranquil little village, caught in a steep cleft in the hills, out of sight of the ugly concrete factories that squat next to the highway. The town is guarded by the ruins of an old Arab fortress, now a small archaeological museum, and tiny cobbled passages twist sharply downhill to the blue-domed 18th-century **Iglesia de San Pedro**. If it's been raining, there's a stunning waterfall at the nearby Cueva Turche, a popular local swimming and picnicking spot.

Requena and and Utiel

Requena and Utiel are in the heart of Valencia's **wine country**, with vines snaking off as far as the eye can see. Requena's **Fiesta de la Vendimia**, celebrated at the end of the grape harvest in late August/early September, is one of the oldest in Spain. The town itself is a prosperous little place, with plane-shaded avenues radiating out from a sinuous medieval core, the Barrio de la Villa. Originally settled by the Arabs, only a single tower, the **Torre del Homenaje**, remains of the original fortress which gave the town its name (Rakkana, meaning 'secure'). It now contains displays on the town's history, and affords fabulous views from the upper levels. There is a smattering of 15th- and 16th-century palaces, an old warehouse that recalls the days when Requena was one of the largest silk-producing centres in Spain, and a fine Gothic church. A 13th-century convent, El Real Convent de Carmen, now contains the municipal museum. In the Plaza de la Villa, you can visit underground caves, **Las Cuevas**, used for wine storage.

Utiel, 13 km west, is less attractive, but you can visit some of the local **bodegas** for tours and tastings. Information is available from the **tourist office** ⓘ *C/Camino 1, T962 170 879, www.utiel.es*.

Listings West of Valencia

Where to stay

€€ Hostal El Vegano
Utiel, T962 172 355.
The only central place to stay here, a simple affair, but with friendly staff and a good, inexpensive restaurant.

€€ Hotel Avenida
C/San Agustín 10, Requena, T962 300 480.
A central, modern hotel, with clean, modest rooms.

€ Casa Petra
C/Purísima 12, Requena, T962 305 509, www.casaruralpetra.com.
A charming little guesthouse, with a handful of rooms in the historic centre.

€ Venta Pillar
Av Pérez Galdós 5, Buñol, T962 500 923, http://posadaventapilar.com.
This classic roadside hotel and restaurant, set in a 17th-century coach inn 4 km from the centre, is one of the only options in Buñol.

Restaurants

There are plenty of old-fashioned café-bars in Buñol along the main street near the Iglesia de San Pedro, which all offer a cheap *menú del día*.

€ Asador Casa Chencho
C/Nicolás Ruiz 16, Utiel, T962 173 156.
Reliable local eatery, serving traditional grilled meats (*carne a la brasa*) plus a good choice of local wines, as well as sandwiches and snacks.

€€ Mesón del Castillo
C/Gómez Ferrer 10, Buñol, T670 2204 83.
Does good meat and seafood cooked over charcoal.

€€ Mesón del Vino
Av Arrabal 11, Requena, T962 300 001.
Head here for local wines and well-cooked regional dishes.

€€ Posada de Águeda
Cra Madrid–Valencia Km 283, Requena, T962 301 418. Closed Sun eve and Mon.
The best restaurant in the area, specializing in local dishes prepared with a touch of creativity.

Alicante &
La Costa Blanca

The Costa Blanca, along with the costas Brava and Sol, is devoted to package tourism on a grand scale. But it's not all skyscraper hotels and 'tea like your mum makes' – some resorts remain refreshingly Spanish, not least among them the energetic city of Alicante.

South of Valencia

a couple of resorts and a prosperous beach town

Cullera

The Costa Blanca proper doesn't start until Dénia, but there are a couple of big seaside towns south of Valencia. The first is Cullera, curled around the steep crag of the Monte del Oro and overlooking a vast, natural bay. The old town has been virtually swallowed up by a bland sprawl of modern apartment blocks but there are 14 km of beaches to compensate. There are **tourist information offices** ⓘ *C/Mar 93, T961 720 974, and beachside at Plaza de la Constitución, T961 731 586, www.culleraturismo.com.*

Gandía

The graceful old town of Gandía is surrounded by orange orchards. Its history is bound up with the fortunes of the Borjas, better known by their Italian name, the Borgias. In 1485, Ferdinand the Catholic gave the town to Rodrigo Borja, who would later become the notorious Pope Alexandro VI. The Spanish branch of the family was less Machiavellian, and the fourth Duke of Gandía, Francisco Borja (1510-1572) was canonized and is the town's patron saint.

The town's most famous sight is the 15th-century **Palacio Ducal de los Borja** ⓘ *C/Santo Duque 1, T962 871 465, www.palauducal.com, Oct-Mar Mon-Sat 1000-1330 and 1500-1830, Apr-Sept Mon-Fri 1000-1330 and 1600-1930, Sun 1000-1330, €6/5, guided tours are available Oct-May Mon-Sat 1100, 1200, 1600, 1700, Jun-Sep 1000, 1200, 1700 and 1800,* where San Francisco was born. The original building was remodelled between the 16th and the 18th centuries, and only the patio retains its original Gothic splendour. The salons are decorated with ornate ceilings, azulejos and marble floors, and one boasts a beautiful frieze depicting the four elements made with ceramics from Manises. Unfortunately, some of the original tiling can't be reproduced as the plants used to make the original Arabic dyes have long been extinct.

The **tourist information office** ⓘ *Av Marqués de Campo, T962 877 788, www. gandiaturismo.com, also at 2 locations near the beach*, has leaflets on various attractive walking and cycling routes around Gandía.

Regular shuttle buses depart from outside the train station in the centre of Gandía for its lively port, **Grao**, 4 km away. **Gandía-Playa** is a big, popular resort with a buzzy nightlife and famously manicured beaches (they get combed by tractors every day).

Listings South of Valencia

Where to stay

€€ La Rochera
Ctra de Barx 79, Marxuquera–Gandía, T962 131 760.
If you've got a car, this delightful B&B a 10-min drive from the town centre offers prettily decorated rooms, a small pool, and views of the hills.

€ El Nido
C/Alcoy 22, Gandía-Playa, T962 844 640.
A good budget choice near the beach, with a cheap restaurant.

Camping

L'Alqueria
T962 840 470, www.lalqueria.com.
Large and well-equipped, located midway between the old town Gandía and the beaches.

Restaurants

€€€ L'Ham
C/Germans Benlliure 22, Grau de Gandía, T962 846 006.
Great local seafood and rice dishes near the port, plus a charming rooftop bar for a cocktail after dinner.

€€ Vins i Mes
C/Salelles 6, Gandía, T962 866 914.
Fantastic wine selection and a wide range of tapas in this stylish local in the centre of the old town.

Transport

Cullera is a 20-min train journey from Valencia. **Gandía** is also on the train line from Valencia, with connections to **Alicante** and **Murcia**.

Around the Cape

the best of the Costa Blanca for those with their own transport

The rocky cape which juts out between Dénia and Altea has some of the prettiest beaches of the Costa Blanca. Many of them are hard to get to without your own transport, which means – at least in terms of the brash Mediterranean Costas – they are comparatively unspoilt.

Dénia

Dénia is a relaxed family resort dotted with colourful villas, and blessed with long sandy beaches. There's a medieval **castle** ⓘ *Av del Cid, T966 420 556, Nov-Mar 1000-*

1300 and 1500-1800, Apr and May 1000-1330 and 1530-1900, Jun 1000-1330 and 1600-1930, Jul and Aug 1000-1330 and 1600-2030 plus night visits, Sep 1000-1330 and 1600-2000 and Oct 1000-1300 and 15000-1830; €3/2, above the town and you make the long scramble up to the top of the peak of Mongó for fantastic views. This wild, windswept area around the peak has been designated a natural park, and there are plenty of hiking trails. The local festival in early July is celebrated with the **Bous A La Mar** (Bulls To The Sea), in which the bulls are chased to the water's edge. There's a **tourist office** ① *C/Dr Manuel Muñoa, T966 422 367, www.denia.net.*

★ Xàbia

Xàbia (Jávea in Castellano) is a delightful old village set on a small hilltop a couple of kilometres back from the sea. The peaceful seaside resort spreads gently around a rocky horseshoe bay cut off by cliffs at either end. It's a low-key place, where, although there are plenty of modern developments, thankfully, high-rise hotels and apartment blocks have been banned. Scores of British and German families have set up home here, and you can pick up *Marmite* in the supermarket or an English book at the friendly bookshop. The **tourist information office** ① *Plaza Almirante Basterreche 24, T965 790 736, www.xabia.org,* runs hiking trips and guided tours in English.

The old pueblo is an immaculate little maze of whitewashed houses and pretty squares. Like most villages of this region, it celebrates its local festival (held in July) with a battle between the Moors and the Christians, which culminates with a spectacular firework show on the seafront. It's a good base for hiking in the **Parque Natural del Montgo** (the tourist office has a series of excellent leaflets describing the various trails) and diving is excellent off the **Cape of San Antonio**, which has been declared a marine reserve to prevent further development. The tourist office has lists of schools offering diving trips.

Calpe

Calpe, around the tip of the cape, is a big, blowsy resort in a stunning natural setting with excellent beaches. The extraordinary rock, the ★**Peñón de Ifach**, which juts sheerly from the sea, was declared a natural reserve to preserve it from the onslaught of tourists. A tunnel has been bored up to the summit, but only 150 visitors are allowed at a time (it's a stiff climb, and takes about two hours). The walk, passing through flower-dotted meadows and over rocky outcrops, is beautiful, and the views from the mirador at the top are breathtaking.

Altea

Altea is a picture-postcard village overlooking the sea. 'Discovered' by artists and hippies in the 1970s, it's still got a mellow atmosphere and craft shops and galleries line its narrow streets. The village is crowned with a rosy church topped with a blue-tiled dome, which overlooks a buzzy square filled with tapas bars. The beach is pebbly and narrow, but still a favourite with families, and there's a craft market along the promenade on Tuesdays.

Benidorm

Benidorm, despite recent efforts to moderate its image, is still the king of package tourism, a mega-resort filled with towering skyscrapers, flashing neon and crammed, sweaty beaches. For years, the only reason to visit was to enjoy a hedonistic holiday of sun, sea and dodgy sangría, although the city has made determined – and successful – efforts to move away from that image, and market itself to families in recent years. It's often seen as a mecca for northern Europeans and it's easy to forget that half the tourists who come here are Spanish.

Listings Around the Cape

Where to stay

€€€€ La Posada del Mar
Plaza Drassanes 2, Dénia, T960 130 856, www.laposadadelmar.com.
A very charming small hotel, set in a beautifully restored 18th-century inn by the port: the best rooms have private terraces with wonderful views. There's an excellent restaurant. Prices drop at least 1, and often 2, categories in low season.

€€€€ SH Villa Gadea
Partida Villa Gadea, Altea, T902 453 015, www.sh-hoteles.com.
This glossy modern complex on a hillside overlooking the sea offers a huge range of facilities, including a spa, outdoor pools, and tennis courts.

€€€€-€€ Hostal El Trovador
C/Cap Negret 15, Altea, T965 841 275.
Simple, friendly, family-run hostal right on the beach, about a 15-min walk from the town centre.

€€€ Parador
Av del Mediterráneo 7, Xàbia, T965 790 200, www.parador.es.
This modern parador is in a magnificent cliff-top location and has a fine restaurant.

€€€-€€ El Rodat
C/La Murciana, Xàbia, T966 470 710, www.elrodat.com.
An elegant hotel and spa, with extensive gardens which contain whitewashed villas, and a split-level pool. It's popular with families and has other facilities including a sauna, gym, and tennis. The restaurant is one of the best in the area.

€€€-€€ Hotel Nou Romá
Av del Cid 3, Dénia, T966 432 843, www.hotelnouroma.com.
An enchanting 3-star boutique hotel in a beautifully restored historic building near the castle. Great restaurant.

€€€-€€ Hotel Porto Calpe
Explanada del Puerto, Calpe, T965 837 322, www.portocalpe.com.
Modern hotel, with comfortable, if bland, rooms, but a spectacular waterfront location by the port.

€€ Hostal Loreto
C/Loreto 12, Dénia, T966 435 419, www.hostalloreto.com.
A charming little hostal in a 400-year-old convent, with simple rooms and a great, central location.

€€ Hotel Castillo
Av del Cid 7, Dénia, T966 421 320, www.hotelcastillodenia.com.
A friendly family-run hotel with comfortable rooms near the beach.

€€ Hotel Javea
C/Pío X 5, Xàbia T965 795 461,
www.hotel-javea.com.
Bright, modern rooms are offered at
this stylish and friendly 2-star hotel,
ideally located just back from the port.
Highly recommended.

€€ Hotel Rosa
C/Marinas 197, Dénia, T965 781 573,
www.hotelrosadenia.com.
A friendly seafront family hotel with a
pool set in gardens, a choice of guest
rooms or bungalows, and a restaurant.

€€ Hotel San Miguel
C/La Mar 65, Altea, T965 840 400.
A delightful spot on the seafront, over
a popular restaurant which serves an
excellent paella. Look out for special offers.

€€ Pensión Marina
Av de la Marina Española 8, Xàbia,
T965 793 139.
Bright rooms right on the beachfront.

€€-€ Hostal L'Anfora
Explanada de Cervantes, Dénia,
T966 430 101.
A simple guesthouse with cosy rooms
overlooking the sea.

€ Hostal Fornet
C/Beniardá 1, Altea, T966 866 314.
One of plenty of budget options
in the old village near the church.

Restaurants

Dénia produces some of the best
prawns in the world. There are lots of
cheaper places along Av Gabriel Miró.

€€€ El Negre
C/Santa Bárbara 4, Altea, T965 841 826.
A traditional restaurant, set in an
elegantly restored mansion in the old
town with a beautiful panoramic terrace.

€€€ Quique Dacosta
Ctra Las Marinas Km 3, Urb, El Poblet,
Dénia, T965 784 179.
One of the very best restaurants in Spain,
named for its famous chef, who prepares
exquisite local produce in the most
innovative ways. Try some of the world's
best prawns here.

€€ El Bodegón
C/Delfín 8, Calpe, T965 830 164.
An atmospheric tavern near the port,
with hanging hams, plenty of charm,
and sophisticated local cuisine.

€€ La Perla de Javea
Av de la Libertad 21, Xàbia, T966 470 772,
www.perladejavea.com.
Fresh seafood and delicious
Medrerreanean rice dishes overlooking
the beach.

€€ La Capella
C/San Pablo 1, Altea, T966 680 484.
Local rice dishes and good grilled
meats served on a pretty terrace.

€€ Los Zapatos
C/Santa María 7, Calpe, T965 831 507.
Imaginative, fresh dishes with a French
twist, and delightful owners.

Tapas bars and cafés

€€ Iberia Gastrobar
C/Sant Buenaventura 9, Xàbia,
T965 996 716.
A charming restaurant specializing
in well-priced tapas dishes, served as
part of a set menu; there's live jazz and
flamenco some nights.

€ El Jamonal de Ramonet
Passeig del Salader 106, Dénia,
T965 785 786.
Great for tapas and *raciones*.

Transport

Boat
More expensive, but a great way of seeing the cape is to take the sightseeing day trip in a glass-bottomed boat from **Dénia** to to **Xàbia** and back (**Mundo Marino**, T966 423 066, www.mundomarino.es, costs €18). The company also offers sunset boat tours and other themed services. The port is the departure point for ferries to the **Balearics** (**Acciona/Trasmediterránea**, T902 454 645, www.trasmediterranea.com, or **Baleària**, www.balearia.com, T902 160 180).

Bus
There are frequent buses (about 20 daily) from Alicante and Valencia along the coast. Express buses with **Alsa**, T902 422 242, www.alsa.es, take about 2½ hrs; avoid local buses which can take 5 hrs (€20 single, €37 return). **Xàbia** is connected by local bus to **Dénia**, 6 times daily during the week but there is no service at weekends.

Train
Dénia is on the main train line south from **Valencia** and on the tram line (TRAM, www.tramalicante.com) from **Alicante** (see below), which stops at **Altea** and **Benidorm**.

Alicante
atmospheric Spanish town with elegant architecture and authentic tapas bars

★Alicante, Valencia's second largest town, is the main gateway for package tours to the Costa Blanca. The coastline is dense with the ugly paraphernalia of hard-core tourism, but the town itself remains authentically and pleasingly Spanish. Elegant, palm-lined boulevards stretch along the seafront, decorated with colourful azulejo tiles and the old town, El Barrio, is an atmospheric huddle of narrow streets. It's packed with buzzy bars and restaurants, and Alicante offers some of the best shopping and nightlife in the whole region.

Sights
Castillo Santa Bárbara ⓘ *Grounds Oct-Mar 1000-2000, Apr-Sep 1000-2200, T966 377 034; MUSA (Museo de Alicante), daily 1000-1430 and 1600-2000, T965 152 969; lift costs €2.70, lift runs 1000-2000; book guided visits, or find times for the theatrical costumed visits in summer at www.castillodesantabarbara.com.* Alicante's biggest monument, the Castillo Santa Bárbara, is an enormous medieval fortress clamped high on the Monte Benacatil. Climb the ancient walls to enjoy tremendous views out to sea. The castle contains the city museum, with exhibits relating its history over the past two millennia. You can reach the castle by lift, which creaks up 205 m (entrance from Aveñida Jovellanos, behind the Playa de Postiguet), or stroll up through the Parque de la Ereneta, a contemporary garden laid out on the west side of the hill.

El Barrio Alicante's old town, known simply as El Barrio, is a cheerfully chaotic scramble of winding passages, stone mansions with flower-filled balconies and a smattering of churches.

The baroque **Concatedral de San Nicolás de Bari** ① *Plaza Abad Penalva 1, T965 212 662, 0730-1300 and 1730-2000, donation requested*, is restrained and elegant, with a single soaring nave below a lofty dome and a quiet cloister. It's dedicated to Alicante's patron saint, but, despite major restoration, it remains a gloomy and oddly unwelcoming place.

Iglesia de Santa María ① *Plaza Santa María, T965 216 026, 1030-1200 and 1830-1930, donation requested*, the oldest church in Alicante, is brighter and prettier. Its twin belltowers and exuberant baroque portal overlook a handsome little square, while the more sombre interior reveals its 15th-century roots. Close by, Alicante's **Museo de Arte Contemporáneo** ① *Plaza Santa María, T965 213 156, www.maca-alicante.es, Tue-Sat 1000-2000, Sun 1000-1400, free*, contains works by Dalí, Picasso, Miró, Tàpies, Chillida and other great Spanish artists of the 20th century, as well as excellent changing exhibitions of contemporary art. Alicante's Museum of Fine Arts, **Museo de Bellas Artes (MUBAG)** ① *C/Gravina 13-15, T965 146 780, www.mubag.com, Tue-Sat 1000-2000, Sun 1000-1400*, is set in a beautifully restored 18th-century building, and houses a permanent collection of artworks from the 16th to the 20th centuries. It also hosts temporary exhibitions.

The **Ayuntamiento (City Hall)** ① *Plaza de Ayuntamiento 1, T965 149 110, Mon-Sat 0900-1400*, is a splendid, baroque building topped with tiled domes. You can tour the sumptuous apartments inside.

One of Alicante's quirkiest museums, the little **Museo de Belenes** ① *C/San Agustín 3, T965 202 232, Jul-Aug Mon 1800-2100, Tue-Fri 1100-1400 and 1600-1800, Sat 1100-1400, Sep-Jun 1000-1400 and 1700-1900, Sat 1000-1400, free*, is devoted to the figurines which decorate nativity cribs. **MARQ (Museo Arqueológico Provincial de Alicante)** ① *Plaza del Doctor Gómez Ulla s/n, T965 159 006, www.marqalicante.com, Tue-Fri 1000-1900, Sat 1000-2030, Sun and holidays 1000-1400*, is a glossy modern archaeology museum stacked with interactive exhibits and high-tech presentations of local history, including the Ibero-Roman city of Lucentum which is being excavated behind the Playa de la Albuferata.

Essential Alicante

Finding your feet

Local buses run between the beaches and the centre of town. Routes are clearly marked at bus stops. The old centre is small and easy to get around on foot. Taxis are usually easy to hail. There's a hop-on, hop-off bus service, the **Turibús**, T902 106 992, www.alicanteturismo.com/turibus, which offers an hour-long circuit of the city for €10/5.

Best time to visit

Alicante gets especially crowded in August, when accommodation can be hard to find, but the summer nightlife is hard to beat. The excellent local festival **Las Hogueras** is held in late June. For further details see page 53.

Beaches The main town beach is the crowded, occasionally grubby, **Playa del Postiguet**. Next up along the coast is **Playa de la Albuferata**, with the ruins of the old Roman settlement of Lucentum behind it. **Playa de la Almadraba** is next, at the foot of the cape, with lots of rocky coves (one is a nudist beach). **Playa San Juan** is a vast, gleaming sandy beach backed by hundreds of hotels, restaurants and discos. There's another great beach on the **Isla de Tabarca** (which belongs to Alicante, although it's easiest to get to from Santa Pola, see below).

Alicante

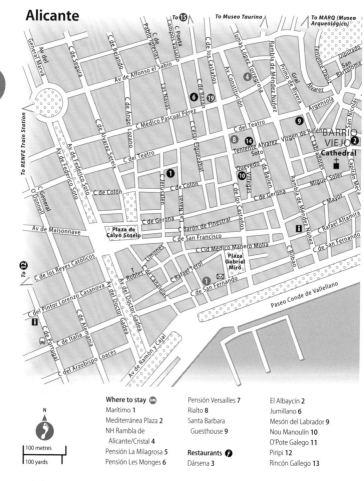

Where to stay
Marítimo **1**
Mediterránea Plaza **2**
NH Rambla de Alicante/Cristal **4**
Pensión La Milagrosa **5**
Pensión Les Monges **6**
Pensión Versailles **7**
Rialto **8**
Santa Barbara Guesthouse **9**

Restaurants
Dársena **3**
El Albaycín **2**
Jumillano **6**
Mesón del Labrador **9**
Nou Manoulín **10**
O'Pote Galego **11**
Piripi **12**
Rincón Gallego **13**

Tourist information

Alicante Tourist Office
Rambla de Méndez Núñez 23, T965 200 000, www.alicanteturismo.com.
There are also branches at the bus station, airport, train station, and the Ayuntamiento. In summer there are additional kiosks at the beaches of San Juan and Postiguet.

Where to stay

€€€ Hotel Mediterránea Plaza
Plaza del Ayuntamiento 6, T965 210 188, www.eurostarsmediterraneaplaza.com.
Handsome, luxury hotel in a converted 18th-century mansion with gym, sauna and a roof terrace with great views. Rooms are stylish but a tad impersonal.

€€ Hotel Marítimo
C/Valdés 13, T965 143 722, www.hmaritimo.com.
Simple hotel in the old quarter with spacious rooms decorated in nautical blue and white.

€€ NH Rambla de Alicante/Cristal
C/López Torregrosa 9, T965 143 659, www.nh-hoteles.es.
Crisp, modern chain hotel with a striking glassy façade; look out for special deals at weekends and in the off season.

€€ Pensión Les Monges
1st floor, C/Monjas 2, T965 215 046, www.lesmonges.es.
This quirky *pensión* has warmly decorated rooms (with a/c for a bit extra), lots of artwork (including a sketch by Dalí), and a great location. Suites with jacuzzi and sauna also available, and you can sun yourself on the panoramic roof terrace. Recommended.

€€ Santa Barbara Guesthouse
C/del Carmen 8, T652 346 614.
Tastefully decorated, simple studios and apartments with a kitchenette, right

Tapas Alicante **1**
Yale **14**

Söda Bar Café **19**

Bars & clubs 🎵
Callejón Pub **17**
Clan Cabaret **15**
Oceanus **4**

in the old quarter. There are wonderful views from the shared roof terrace.

€ Hotel Rialto
C/Castaños 30, T965 206 433.
Basic, immaculate rooms with a/c, with friendly staff, centrally located in the old quarter.

€ Pensión La Milagrosa
C/Villavieja 8, T965 216 918, www.lamilagrosa.eu.
A choice of simply decorated rooms or apartments, plus a delightful breakfast terrace.

€ Pensión Versailles
C/Villavieja 3, T965 214 593.
A good family-run budget choice, with spotless rooms set around a plant-filled courtyard and a shared kitchen in the heart of the buzzy Barrio Viejo.

Restaurants

€€€ Dársena
Pso del Puerto, T965 207 399, www.darsena.com.
There are more than 100 different rice-based dishes to choose from in this elegant, classic restaurant overlooking the port.

€€ Jumillano
C/César Elguezábal 62-64, T965 212 964. Closed Jul, Aug, Sep and Sun.
A classic, traditional restaurant which was founded in 1941 and is decorated with paintings by local artists and plenty of taurine memorabilia. Great tapas, or delicious local dishes in the restaurant.

€€ Nou Manoulín
C/Villegas 3, T965 200 368.
An enormously popular, brick-lined restaurant with classic regional dishes

and a good-value *menú del día* at around €15. If you don't want to go the whole hog, there's an excellent, permanently crowded tapas bar on the ground floor.

€€ O'Pote Galego
Plaza Santísima Faz 6, T965 208 084.
A charming Gallego restaurant with a terrace overlooking a pretty little square behind the Ayuntamiento. The emphasis is on fish, either simply grilled over charcoal, or served with different sauces.

€€ Piripi
C/Oscar Esplá 30, T965 227 940.
Dine on traditional Levante cuisine prepared with the freshest local ingredients, or just sit at the bar for a fabulous range of tapas and wines. The lunchtime *menú del día* is a great bargain.

€€ Rincón Gallego
C/Pórtico Ansaldo 1, T965 219 616.
Tasty Gallego specialities – lots of seafood, especially *pulpo* (octopus), washed down with sharp white wine. Enjoy tapas at the bar, if you don't want a full dinner.

€ El Albaycín
C/San Nicolás 22.
Great, old-fashioned, Granada-style tasca, which serves a free tapa with drinks, plus hearty *raciones* of traditional favourites.

Tapas bars and cafés
The tapas bars at the **El Nou Manolín** and **Piripiri** (run by brothers) are popular and excellent.

Mesón del Labrador
C/Labradores19, T965 204 846.
A classic on the Alicantino tapas scene, a traditional old stalwart serving a wide range of tapas and *raciones*.

Tapas Alicante
C/Felipe Bergé, T965 145 095.
Great value and delicious tapas: also
a good place for breakfast or brunch.

Yale
C/Teniente Alvárez Soto 6, T965 204 344.
Just a handful of tables, but a wonderful
array of tapas and *montaditos* (slices of
crusty baguette with different toppings).
There's also a pretty terrace for fine days.

Bars and clubs

Nightlife in Alicante is concentrated
in 2 main areas. '**La Zona**' (behind
Explanada on the streets around
Av de Ramón y Cajal) is most popular
with teenagers and students. But the
wildest, noisiest nightlife is in **El Barrio**,
the old part of town around the
Cathedral of San Nicolas. In summer,
head for the beaches, especially **Playa
San Juan**, for countless outdoor bars
and clubs. Many disco-bars are open
Thu-Sat only. Check out *Alicante Out*
(Spanish only, www.alicanteout.com)
for listings.

Callejón Pub
Plaza Quijano, 6, T647 269 978. Thu-Sat.
One of the stalwarts of Alicante's
nightlife, with inexpensive drinks
and a lively atmosphere. DJ sets
and theme nights.

Clan Cabaret
*C/Capitán Segarra 16, T965 210 003,
www.clancabaret.com.*
Popular, long-standing bar, with
live music, DG events, dramatic
monologues, etc.

Oceanus
Muelle de Levante s/n, T965 1451 97.
Restaurant, bar and club with
magnificent sea views.

Söda Bar Café
*C/ Médico Pascual Pérez 8, T965 200 722.
Wed-Sun.*
Popular café-bar, with DJ sets most nights.

Festivals

24 Jun Las Hogueras (**Les Fogueres**),
Alicante's biggest and best festival,
is held on the feast of San Juan. The
Hogueras are the massive sculptures
which, despite taking months of hard
work to build, end up in the flames.
Picasso, Dalí and Miró have designed
them in the past – all turned to ashes
along with the rest.

Transport

Air
Alicante-Elche Airport, T902 404 704,
www.aena.es, is 12 km from the centre
at El Altet. As the main gateway to the
Costa Blanca, it is one of the busiest
airports in Spain, used by a number of
no-frills airlines. It has 2 terminals and
plenty of services, including shops,
restaurants, a tourist information office,
post office, ATMs and car rental offices.
There are taxis (€20-22 to the centre) and
buses to the the main bus centre on Calle
Portugal from outside the Arrivals hall
(llegadas) every 20 mins between 0530
and midnight (€2.70). For information on
flights, see page 74.

Bus
The main bus station is at Puerto
de Alicante, Muelle de Poniente s/n,
T965 130 700.
    For the **Playa de San Juan**, take bus
Nos 9, 21, 22, 21C, 21N; for the **Playa de
Alburefeta**, take bus Nos 9, 21, and 22.
Buses run at least every 15 mins and
on summer weekends buses serve the
string of discos north of Alicante all

night. For information call T965 140 936, www.subus.es.

There are bus services along the **Costa Blanca**, and to **Granada**, **Almería**, **Barcelona**, **Jaén**, **Málaga**, **Sevilla**, **Madrid** and **Valencia**. International services to **London**, **Paris** and many other destinations with **Eurolines**.

Car hire
There are plenty of places offering car rental, both at the airport and in town (mostly by the train station). Try **Avis**, by the station at Av de Salamanca 1, T965 136 258, www.avis.es; **Budget**, also at Av de Salamanca 1, T965 682 779, www.budget.es; and **Atesa**, at the airport, T902 100 101, www.atesa.es.

Taxi
Tele Taxi, T965 101 611, www.teletaxi alicante.es, or **Radio Taxi**, T965 252 511.

Train
The tram runs along the **Costa Blanca** between **Alicante** and **Dénia**, stopping at the popular beaches at **San Juan**, **Benidorm**, **Altea**, **Calpe**, **Gata** and **Dénia**. For info see www.tramalicante.es (also in English), or call T900 720 472.

The RENFE train station is at Av Salamanca, T902 320 320, www.renfe.com. There are **Euromed** and **Talgo** services to **Valencia**, **Barcelona** and **Murcia**, and AVE trains to **Madrid**. Local trains connect **Alicante** with **Elche**, **Orihuela**, **Xátiva** and **Murcia**.

South of Alicante

low-key sights away from the main beach resorts

South of Alicante, there are more resorts and (slightly) quieter beaches along the coast. Inland, the palm forests and gardens of Elche offer shade and tranquility, and the little town of Orihuela hides a beautiful baroque core.

Santa Pola and Isla de Tabarca
Santa Pola is another overgrown fishing village with a ring of concrete apartment blocks. The attractive port has a small fishing fleet and offers ferry links to the tiny island of Tabarca, 3.5 km out to sea. The island belongs to Alicante, but more ferries make the short trip from Santa Pola. It's a favourite with birdwatchers and divers – heavenly out of season, but in summer it can get horribly crowded. The former **Casa del Gobernador** (Governor's House) is now a pretty little hotel.

Elx/Elche
Elche, in a fertile plain 22 km southwest of Alicante, is a pristine modern city of broad avenues with a tiny old core. It's famous for three things: palm trees, a medieval mystery play and an ancient sculpture of a woman, the fourth- or fifth-century BC Dama de Elche. The palm trees were first planted by the Phoenicians, and are still the city's biggest industry. The palms produce dates, but the cultivators make even more of a profit from their fronds, which form the crosses used throughout Spain on Palm Sunday (and are often kept as charm against lightning). The beautiful botanical gardens of the **Huerto del Cura** ① *Porta de la Morera, T961 451 936, http://jardin.huertodelcura.com, €5/3*, laid out in the late

19th century, are a delight to explore, and contain some of the oldest palm trees, including one that's more than 150 years old.

Elche's medieval mystery play, the *Misteri d'Elx*, is held each year on 14-15 August in the 18th-century **Basílica de Santa María**. If you miss it, there's a small **museum** ⓘ *C/Major de la Villa 25, T965 453 464, Tue-Sat 1000-1400 and 1500-1800, Sun 1000-1400 (audio-visual shows are at 1015, 1100, 1145, 1230, 1315, 1515, 1600 and 1645), €3/1, free on Sun*, dedicated to its history close by.

In 1897, the **Dama de Elche** was discovered in La Alcudia, 2 km south of the town centre. It's easily the most famous piece of ancient art in Spain, and the sculpture of the woman with the inscrutable gaze (Elche's answer to the *Mona Lisa*) now has pride of place in Madrid's archaeological museum. There's a copy of it, along with finds from prehistoric, Phoenician and Roman times, in the **Museo Arqueológico** ⓘ *Palacio Altamira, T965 453 603, Tue-Sat 1000-1800, Sun 1000-1500, €3/1.50*, just north of the cathedral.

It's also possible to visit the **excavations** of La Alcudia, where there's an excellent **museum** ⓘ *Ctra Dolores 2 km, T966 611 506, Tue-Sat 1000-2000, Sun 1000-1500, €5/2*, devoted to the history of the settlement, and a video guide system around the site.

Orihuela

Orihuela is one of those Spanish towns which don't look much on the outskirts but blossom on a closer viewing. It has an immaculate medieval centre stuffed full of reminders of its glorious past. In 1488, it was important enough for the Catholic Kings to hold court here, and mansions, churches and bridges attest to its former affluence.

The 14th-century **cathedral** ⓘ *Mon-Fri 1000-1400 and 1600-1830, Sat 1000-1400, free*, is small but perfectly formed in the Catalan Gothic tradition, with twisting columns and a pretty cloister (moved here brick by brick from an old convent in 1942). The nearby archbishop's palace contains a museum with a rich collection of religious paintings, including works by Ribera, Velázquez and Morales. There's also a **tourist office** ⓘ *Plaza de la Soledad 1, T965 304 656*.

The charming **Iglesia de Santiago Apóstol**, which contains sculptures by the Murcian artist Salzillo. Above the portal are the emblems of the 'Catholic Kings' (Isabella and Fernando) who founded it. Look out for the whimsical **Iglesia de Santa Justa y Rufina**, with a belltower topped with a fleet of gargoyles.

The most elaborate monument in Orihuela is the **Colegio Diocesano Santo Domingo**, which became a university in 1569, and is now a school, is set around two graceful cloisters. You might be able to visit the charming old refectory, decorated with faded azulejo tiling, and the main church, which is a breathless, gilded swirl of baroque cherubs and ornamentation.

There are two small museums dedicated to Orihuela's biggest festivals: the **Museo del Semana Santa**, with exhibits on the Holy Week processions, and the **Museo de la Reconquista**, with costumes and photos from the annual **Battle of the Moors and the Christians** which takes place every July. Peek into the pretty 19th-century **Teatro Circo** and take a stroll around Orihuela's cool palm grove, **El Palmeral**, on the outskirts of town.

Where to stay

€€€€ Huerto del Cura
Porta de la Morera 14, Elche, T966 612 050, www.huertodelcura.com.
A modern hotel opposite the beautiful botanic garden, with bungalows scattered around the beautiful palm grove. It has extensive sports facilities, even its own Zen temple, and offers excellent weekend deals.

€€ Hostal Rey Teodomiro
Av Teodomiro 10, Orihuela, T965 300 349.
Friendly small hotel with traditionally decorated rooms in the town centre.

€€ Jardín Milenio
Prolongación de Curtidores s/n, Elche, T966 612 033, www.restaurantecasacorro.com.
Set amid the ancient palms, this peaceful modern hotel is just a 10-min walk from the historic quarter.

€ Casa Corro
Avda del Dr García Rogel 23, Elche, T965 302 963, www.hotelmilenio.com.
Simple, old-fashioned rooms on the edge of town: attached to a traditional restaurant, run by 3 sisters, which serves great value local cuisine.

Restaurants

There are plenty of cheap places to eat in Orihuela around the Av Teodomiro.

€€€ Huerto del Cura
Elche, see Where to stay.
Has one of the best restaurants in town, if you've got plenty of cash to blow.

€€ Restaurante Dátil de Oro
Passeig de l'Estació s/n, Elche, T965 453 415.
Set under palm trees in the pretty municipal park and serves good local rice-based dishes in the mid-range price category.

€ Casa Pepe
C/Pedro Maza 2, Orihuela, T966 269 836.
Lively, local favourite, good for traditional local dishes and tapas.

€ Mesón El Tozal
C/Arbres 22, Elche.
There's a tasty *menú del día*.

Inland from the Costa Blanca

dramatic hilltop towns, crowded in high season

There are some engaging mountain towns in Valencia's interior to withdraw to if you fancy a break from the coast. Hill-top Guadalest is the most striking, but also by far the most touristy, but lovely Xàtiva provides a welcome respite from the heat and bustle. Every village celebrates its local fiesta, but the best-known is Alcoy's Battle of the Moors and the Christians.

Guadalest

Guadalest is a beautiful medieval village perched alarmingly on a pinnacle. The rock is a natural fortress, accessed via a tunnel, and the views from the lofty Plaza de Castillo are staggering. Its proximity to Benidorm – less than 30 km – means

ON THE ROAD

The Moor the merrier

According to local legend, the costumed parades and mock battles between the Moors and the Christians began when Felipe II and the Princess Isabel Clara Eugenia stopped off at Dénia's castle and were subjected to a fake ambush by men in Turkish costume. Suddenly, an army kitted out in Christian attire appeared from nowhere to chase the marauders away. The king thought it was a good joke and mock battles are now an intrinsic part of the local festivals of the Costa Blanca.

that tour buses disgorge thousands of visitors in an unending stream. Catch it out of season, or as early in the day as possible, as the mist lifts from the valley below. If you've got your own transport, stop off for a swim at the **Fuentes del Algar**, a string of waterfalls and natural pools hidden away in the forest near the small town of **Callosa d'en Sarrià**. There are few accommodation options in Guadalest itself, but there are plenty of *casas rurales* in the area, as well as a couple of *pensiones* in the nearby village of **Benimantell** (see page 58).

Xàtiva/Játiva

Xàtiva, a tranquil town surrounded by olive groves and vines, has a sprinkling of old stone mansions and is topped with a castle. Set about 60 km south of Valencia, and about 30 km inland from Dénia, it's a popular weekend retreat. The town is the birthplace of two Borgia popes, **Calixtus III** and his nephew **Alexander VI**, as well as the painter **José de Ribera** (1591-1652).

It's a hot and dusty climb up to the **castle** ⓘ *Subida de Castillo s/n, mid-Mar to mid-Oct Tue-Sun 1000-1900, mid-Oct to mid-Mar Tue-Sun 1000-1800, €2.10/1.10*, but worth it for the stunning views. On the way stop off at the Romanesque **Ermita de Sant Feliu**, with some striking medieval paintings inside. Just a few stones survive of the Castell Menor, but the Castell Major is largely intact. This is where the Bishop of Urgell, a pretender to the throne of Aragón, was imprisoned by Ferdinand I. You can stroll along the battlements and old walls which snake across the peak. At weekends, costumed actors recreate some of the most important events in an entertaining guided visit.

Back down in the old town, there are still a handful of noble mansions (mainly in private hands and closed to visitors), but much of Xàtiva was destroyed by Felipe V – three times. The townspeople have punished him posthumously in the **Museo de Almudín** ⓘ *C/Corretgería 46, T962 276 597, 15 Jun-15 Sep Tue-Fri 0930-1430, Sat-Sun 1000-1430, 16 Sep-14 Jun Tue-Fri 1000-1400 and 1600-1800, Sat-Sun 1000-1430, €2.10*, by turning his portrait upside down. The museum also contains Arabic ceramics and a beautiful artesonado ceiling, as well as works by Ribera.

Alcoi/Alcoy

Alcoi is a nondescript working town, but each year on the feast of **Saint George** (Sant Jorge, 23 April), it hosts the biggest and most dramatic enactment of the battle of the **Moros y Cristianos**, see box, page 57. St George came to the rescue during the Battle of Alcoy in 1276, and the festival has been celebrated ever since. The best costumes make it into the town museum, the **Museo Alcoyano de la Fiesta** ⓘ *C/San Miguel 60, Tue-Sat 1100-1400 and 1600-1900, Sun and holidays 1100-1400, €3*, which has lots of exhibits, models and videos if you miss the real thing.

Listings Inland from the Costa Blanca

Where to stay

€€€€ Hostería de Mont Sant
Ctra de Castillo s/n, Xàtiva, T962 275 081, www.mont-sant.com.
For a real treat, stay here. Set in a former monastery with pool, gardens and a fine restaurant.

€€ El Trestellador
Benimantell, T965 885 221.
A welcoming hostal which also has a good cheap restaurant.

€€ Hotel Murta
C/Angel Lacalle s/n, Xàtiva, T962 276 611, www.hotelmurta.com.
A modest choice near the football stadium.

Transport

From **Xàtiva** bus services travel to **Gandia** and **Valencia**. There are regular train services from Xàtiva to **Valencia** (at least 8 daily, about 1 hr), **Alicante**, **Murcia** and **Cartagena**.

The easiest way to get to **Guadalest** is to take a tour (information at the Benidorm tourist office). A single daily bus services, **Llorente Bus**, T965 854 322, www.llorentebus.es, departs Mon-Fri from **Benidorm**.

Inland
Murcia

The autonomous Community of Murcia is often overlooked in the race for the more glamorous resorts of Andalucía or Valencia, and it's regularly the butt of jokes by other Spaniards. But, with the rising popularity of 'rural tourism', Murcia's long-neglected interior is finally opening up to visitors. The handsome towns of Lorca and Caravaca de la Cruz brim with opulent monuments to their illustrious past, but there are scores of sleepy, castle-topped villages with unusual local fiestas that are just beginning to feature on tourist itineraries. Best of all are the green slopes of the Sierra de Espuña, a natural park popular with hikers and birdwatchers. Not to mention the capital, a prosperous, engaging little city with a striking baroque cathedral and great nightlife.

Murcia city

laid-back commercial hub with a lively cultural scene

★Murcia is a truly delightful, deeply Spanish little city, where the *paseo* and the *tapeo* are an intrinsic part of everyday life. The superb baroque cathedral is its grandest monument, but the city is best appreciated sitting out on one of the numerous flower-filled squares, tucking into tapas or enjoying a drink. The centre of Murcia is small and easy to negotiate on foot.

Sights
Murcia's cathedral ① *Plaza Cardenal Belluga 1, T968 221 371*, was begun in 1394 on the ruins of the mosque, and is built in a surprisingly harmonious hotchpotch of styles. The Gothic Puerta de los Apóstoles is the oldest surviving portal, but the façade was transformed in the 18th century and is covered in exuberant baroque sculpture, topped with an elaborate belltower (which you can climb for tremendous

BACKGROUND
Murcia

Murcia was founded in 831 by Abd-Al-Rahman on the banks of the Río Segura, which irrigated the surrounding *vega*, or pastureland, ensuring the city's prosperity. In 1243, it fell to Alfonso X, and reached the height of its influence in the 17th and 18th centuries, when its most splendid baroque monuments were built.

views). Inside, there are several beautiful chapels, of which the Capilla de los Vélez, encrusted with florid plateresque decoration, and the Capilla de Junterones, are the finest. The cathedral's greatest treasure is the heart of Alfonso X 'the wise', who died in Seville, but had his heart sent back to Murcia to show his great love for the city. There's a museum, with paintings and sculpture, a frieze from a Roman sarcophagus, and an enormous gilded monstrance used in the Semana Santa processions.

The cathedral overlooks the Plaza Cardenal Belluga, a great place for tapas on the terrace, flanked on the opposite side by the elegant 18th-century **Palacio Episcopal**. On the other side of the cathedral, narrow **Calle Trapería** follows the route of the main street of Arabic Murcia. On the right is the sumptuous **Casino** ⓘ *T968 215 399, www.realcasinomurcia.com, 1030-1900, visits cost €5, €3 concessions for non-members*, an eye-popping turn-of-the-20th-century monument to eclecticism, with a spectacular ballroom, a restaurant (also open to the public), and a ladies' powder room with primping nymphs floating across the ceiling.

Calle Trapería culminates in the Plaza de Santo Domingo, another favourite for the *tapeo*. The university stands just to the east of the square, and it's one of the liveliest neighbourhoods for nightlife. A short walk away is Murcia's **Museo de Bellas Artes (MUBAM)** ⓘ *C/Obsipos Frutos 8, T968 239 346, Mon-Fri 1000-1400 and 1700-2000, Sat 1100-1400 and 1700-2000, Sun and public hols 1100-1400, closed afternoons in Jul and Aug*, with a collection of minor paintings and sculpture, and often interesting temporary exhibitions.

> **Tip...**
> The **Murcia Tourist Card**, which you can purchase in the tourist office, is valid for 24, 48 or 72 hours (costs €12, €18 and €21 respectively, with discounts for children, and a 5% discount when purchased online at www.turismodemurcia.es) and includes free entrance to most museums, plus discounts at shops and attractions.

Just north of the Plaza de Santo Domingo is the **Monasterio de Santa Clara de la Real**, where you can buy cakes from the cloistered nuns, or admire the 18th-century church and delicate Mudéjar cloister. The **museum** ⓘ *Tue-Sat 1000-1300 and 1600-1830, €3*, contains an excellent collection of Islamic art. Further north, the interesting **Museo Arqueológico** ⓘ *C/Alfonso X, T968 234 602, winter Tue-Sat 1000-1400 and 1700-2000, Sun 1100-1400, summer Tue-Sat 1000-1400, free*, has a collection of finds from archaeological digs all over Murcia.

Museo Salzillo ① *Plaza San Augustín 3, T968 291 893, www.museosalzillo.com, winter Tue-Sat 1000-1700, Sun 1100-1400, summer Mon-Sat 1000-1400, €5/4,* displays the extraordinarily detailed *pasos* (floats) created by Francisco Salzillo (1707-1783) used in Murcia's famous Semana Santa processions. The figures are astonishingly

Murcia

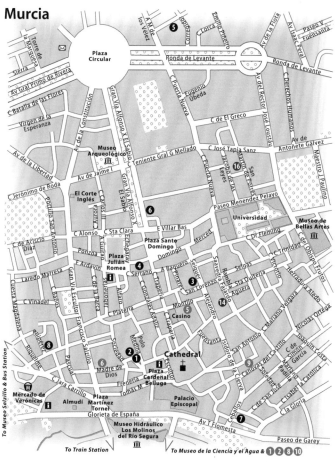

lifelike and are displayed in an ornate baroque church along with a collection of *belenes*, the figurines used in Christmas Nativity scenes.

Close to the Ayuntamiento, an Arabic grain warehouse, or **Palacio del Almudí**, was splendidly rebuilt in the 17th century and is now used for temporary art exhibitions. Close by is the **Mercado de las Verónicas**, one of the prettiest of Murcia's many produce markets. Behind it is delightful **Plaza de las Flores**, one of the liveliest squares in Murcia.

On the opposite bank of the river are two museums. **Museo Hidráulico Los Molinos del Río Segura** ⓘ *C/Molinos 1, T968 358 600, www.molinosdelrio.org, Mon-Sat 1000-1400 and 1700-2000; closed Sat in Jul and Aug*, is set in slickly refurbished watermills on the river, and uses multimedia exhibits to describe their mechanism and history.

The nearby **Museo de la Ciencia y el Agua** ⓘ *Plaza de la Ciencia, T968 211 998, www.cienciayagua.org, Tue-Sat 1000-1400 and 1630-1900, Sun 1100-1400, closed Sat-Sun in summer, €1.50, planetario €1*, is modern and crisply designed. It's geared towards children, and does a fantastic job of making education fun, with lots of great interactive exhibits and a kid-friendly mini-planetarium.

Listings Murcia city *map p61*

Tourist information

There are 2 tourist offices: Plaza Cardenal Belluga, T968 358 600, www.turismodemurcia.es; and C/Santa Clara (behind the Teatro Romea), T968 222 781. For provincial information go to www.murciaturistica.com.

Where to stay

Murcia's hotels are overwhelmingly geared towards business travellers, offering little in the way of charm. However, this does mean that you'll find excellent weekend deals.

€€€ Hotel Conde de Floridablanca
C/Corbalán 7, T968 214 626, www.hoteles-catalonia.es.
Plush, central hotel in an 18th-century townhouse with a modern annexe. Prices can drop to as little as €45 at weekends.

€€€ Tryp Rincón de Pepe
C/Apóstoles 34, T968 212 239, www.melia.com.
Large, modern rooms and an excellent bar (see below) and fine, classically elegant, expensive restaurant. It also offers excellent weekend deals (**€€-€**).

€€ Hesperia Murcia
C/Madre de Dios 4, T968 217 789, www.hesperia.es.
Modern, functional hotel close to the cathedral, offering modest rooms and a fantastic location.

€€ Hotel Universal Pacoche
C/Cartagena 30, T968 217 605, www.universalpacoche.es.
A classic, old-fashioned Spanish hotel with friendly staff near the Floridablanca gardens.

€€ La Huertanica
C/Infantes 5, T968 217 668, http://hotelahuertanica.es.

A small hotel with good-sized, modestly decorated rooms and a restaurant.

€€-€ Hotel Casa Emilio
C/Alameda Colón 9, T968 220 631.
Simple, affordable rooms close to the Jardín de Floridablanca.

€ Pensión Segura
Plaza de Camachos 19, T968 211 281.
Just across the river, this is a plain and simple budget option with rooms decorated with brown chintz and friendly staff.

Restaurants

Many of Murcia's best and best-known restaurants are attached to hotels – if you want to eat well and cheaply, follow the locals and eat at the city's excellent tapas bars.

€€€ Acuario
Plaza Puxmarina 1, T968 219 955.
Delicious regional cuisine, prepared with a creative touch. There's a reasonable *menú de degustación* for €33.

€€€ NH Rincón de Pepe
See Where to stay.
Is considered one of the best in town.

€€ El Churra
C/Obispo Sancho Dávila 14, T968 271 522, www.elchurra.net.
A classic local favourite, serving tasty Murcian dishes, with a good *menú* at €15 and a popular tapas bar.

€€ La Huertanica
See Where to stay.
Has a good restaurant.

€€ Malena Restobar
Plaza Puxmarina 2, T868 044 108.
Big, stylish bistro near the cathedral, with tasty Argentinean and Italian food and friendly service.

Tapas bars and cafés

Café de Ficciones
C/Fuensanta 5, T968 078 565.
Inviting bookshop/video club/bar and café, where you can relax over coffee and cakes, or join in the regular themed parties and cultural events.

El Arco
C/Arco de Santo Domingo, T968 219 767.
A fancy, designer café opposite the Teatre Romea with tables on the square for lingering over coffee or breakfast. Occasional live music.

Heladería Chambi
Av Alfonso X El Sabio 2.
Popular café serving superb home-made ice cream, plus refreshing *horchata* and *granizados*.

La Muralla
At the hotel Tryp Rincón de Pepe (see Where to stay, above).
Incorporating part of the old Moorish walls, this is an upmarket tapas bar and café.

La Pequeña Taberna Típica
C/General Margallo s/n, T968 219 840.
A charming little tavern, this serves delicious creative cuisine in a series of set menus (including a great-value lunch menu) in the medium to high price bracket, as well excellent tapas.

La Tapa
Plaza de las Flores 13, T968 211 317.
One of many tapas bars on the delightful Plaza de las Flores, this is always jam-packed. Good *croquetas*.

Bars and clubs

Murcia is pretty lively for a city its size. Most of the action takes place around the university; check out the bars along

C/Doctor Fleming and around the Plaza Universidad. There are more bars along C/Alfaro, near the Plaza Julian Romea.

El Taller
C/Saavedra Fajardo 3, T968 223 533.
A swish, airy local bar with DJ sessions.

La Puerta Falsa
C/San Martín de Porres 5, T968 200 484, www.lapuertafalsa.com.
Live jazz, tertulias and a laid-back atmosphere.

Shopping

Murcia is an affluent little city and there are plenty of fancy fashion and interior shops all over town.

For one-stop shopping, the department store **El Corte Inglés** has 2 vast premises opposite each other on the Gran Via Salzillo. To see what local crafts are on offer, visit **El Centro de Artesanía** (C/Francisco Rabal 8, T968 284 585, www.murciaartesana.com).

Transport

Air
Murcia-San Javier Airport, www.aena.es, is at San Javier, near the Mar Menor, 48 km from the city. A relatively small airport, it has a few services including ATMs, car rental offices and cafés. There is no public transport to the airport, but there is a taxi rank (€70-80 to the centre of Murcia City). For information on flights, see page 74.

Bus
The bus station is on the east of the city centre at C/Sierra de la Pila 3, T968 292 211, www.estaciondeautobusesde murcia.com. There are regular services to **Barcelona**, **Madrid**, **Málaga**, **Granada**, **Córdoba** and **Sevilla** and most other major Spanish cities, plus local buses to **Aguilas**, **Lorca**, **Totana**, **Moratalla**, **Cartagena** and **Mazarrón**.

Train
There are direct **Euromed** and **Talgo** trains down the coast from **Barcelona** via **Valencia** and **Alicante**. Regional trains from Alicante are cheaper and almost as fast. There are direct trains to **Madrid** (about 4 a day), and local services to **Cartagena** and **Lorca**. The train station is 2 km from the city centre; take bus Nos C1 or C5.

Southwest of Murcia
pretty market town known for its Semana Santa celebrations

Lorca
Lorca is attractively huddled under the ruins of a castle, and has been an important settlement since the time of the Visigoths. Its **Semana Santa** celebrations are the most lavish in Murcia, and it's a lively little place all year round. Baroque churches and mansions dot the narrow streets, and the elegant squares are perfect for an indolent long lunch or some tapas in the evenings. Rocked by an earthquake in 2011, works are still underway across the city to repair the damage. The heart of the town is the **Plaza de España**, presided over by the Ayuntamiento (formerly a prison which explains the allegories of Charity and Justice which surmount it) and the exuberantly baroque **Colegiata de San Patricio** ① *Mon-Fri 1100-1300 and 1630-1830, Sat-Sun 1100-1300, free.*

One of the most eye-catching of Lorca's many mansions is the **Palacio de los Guevara**, which now houses the **tourist office**, and is better known as the 'House of Columns' for the ornate twisting pillars at the entrance. Lorca was an important craft centre for centuries, and the **Centro de Artesanía** next door displays some of the finest. There's another extravagant Renaissance mansion on the corner of the Plaza Vicente, which is attached to a single Roman column, a former marker on the old Roman Via Herculea.

It's a long, hot climb up to the **castle**, built on the ruins of the Moorish fortress after the Reconquest, which is now a luxurious parador (see below).

Totana

Totana, 40 km southwest of Murcia, is a prosperous ceramic-producing town in the foothills of the Sierra de Espuña. In the surrounding hills are the curious *pozos de nieve*, the stone snow wells which were used right up until the beginning of the 20th century. There's a **tourist office** ⓘ *Plaza Constitución 1, T968 418 153, www.turismo.totana.es.*

Listings Southwest of Murcia

Where to stay

€€€ Parador de Lorca
Lorca, T968 406 047, www.parador.es.
Remnants of a genuine medieval castle have been topped, rather bizarrely, with a modern interpretation of a medieval castle at this parador. But the views are tremendous and there's a good restaurant too.

€€ Monasterio de Santa Eulalia
Paraje de la Santa, Ctra Totana–Aledo Km 7, Totana, T968 487 004, www. monasterio santaeulalia.com.
Lovely rural hotel with surprisingly affordable accommodation in a gorgeous setting in the Sierra Espuña. Extras include a gym, pool and restaurant.

€€ Sercotel Spa Jardines de Lorca
Alameda de Rafael Méndez, Lorca, T968 470 599, www.hoteljardinesdelorca.com.
Fancy modern hotel with an outdoor pool, spa, and fantastic off-season and weekend deals.

€ Hotel Félix
Av Fuerzas Armadas, Lorca, T968 467 650, www.hotelfelix.es.
Charming, modest hotel near the train station, with immaculate rooms, friendly service and a good-value restaurant specializing in seafood.

€ Pensión Camioneros
Ctra N340 Km 287, Totana.
A truck-drivers' favourite on the edge of town (which can be noisy).

€ Pensión del Carmen
Rincón de los Valientes 3, Lorca, T968 466 459.
Central, spotless but basic. It's set above a wonderfully old-fashioned restaurant, see below.

Restaurants

In Lorca, you'll find upmarket restaurants at the parador and at the **Sercotel Spa Jardines de Lorca** (see above).

€€ La Cava
C/La Cava 30, Lorca, T968 441 813.
This offers creative Mediterranean cuisine.

€€ La Santa
*Paraje de la Santa, Ctra Totana–
Aledo Km 7, T968 487 004, www.
monasteriosantaeulalia.com.*
A tranquil spot for a long lunch: see the
Hotel Monasterio de Santa Eulalia, above.

€€ Los Cazorlos
Ctra de Aguilas 250, T968 471 060, Lorca.
A classic roadside inn specializing in local
dishes, with a wide-ranging menu.

€ Rincón de los Valientes
*C/Rincón de los Valientes 3, Lorca,
T968 466 459.*
Classic, old-fashioned restaurant below
the Pensión del Carmen (see above),
with decent home-cooking and a cheap
menú del día.

Transport

There are 2 train stations in **Lorca**, both
a short walk from the historic centre,
although **Lorca Sotullena** is slightly
closer than **Lorca San Diego**. The
latter will be the station for high-speed
services to Almería in Andalucía when
the line is completed. There are regular
regional trains to Murcia and Alicante.
The bus station (T968 441 107) is right
next to Lorca Sotullena train station on
C/Carruajes, and offers regular services
to **Murcia**, **Cartagena** and some of the
smaller villages. There's also a daily bus
service to **Granada**.

From Totana there are regional
trains to **Murcia** and **Aguilas** and local
buses from the adjacent bus station to
Murcia, **Mazarrón** and **Lorca** (for bus
information, call T968 425 427).

★ Sierra de Espuña
The Sierra de Espuña is Murcia's most dramatic natural park, a surprisingly lush
wilderness of pine-clad mountains watched over by eagles and vultures. It's
a paradise for hikers and climbers, and the **Centro de Interpretación** ⓘ *inside
the park, T968 431 430, www.sierraespuna.com*, has maps and leaflets describing
walking routes and the park's flora and fauna.

The best base for the park is the little town of **Alhama de Murcia**, about 2.5 km
from the park border, which has a ruined Arabic castle and plenty of tour operators
running walking, biking, horse riding and nature trips into the park (information
from the tourist information office).

Caravaca de la Cruz
Caravaca de la Cruz is an impressive sight, a golden city set against pale mountains.
High above it looms the dramatic 15th-century Templar castle, still contained by
sturdy walls studded with towers. The fortified citadel contains the city's greatest
treasure: the **Basílica de la Vera Cruz** ⓘ *Tue-Sun 1000-1400 and 1600 and 1900 (until
2000 in summer), €4/2, includes audio guide and admission to museum.* According to
legend, a cross borne by two angels appeared to the Moorish king of Valencia in
1231. The ornate baroque chapel was built to house the relic, but it was lost during

the Civil War, and the Vatican sent a sliver of the True Cross to replace it. The miracle is commemorated annually on 3 May, when the Cross is processed through the streets and 'bathed'. In 2008, Pope Benedict XVI declared Caravaca de la Cruz the fifth Holy City in the Catholic faith, and granted it the right to celebrate a Jubilee Year in perpetuity. The next will be held in 2017.

Caravaca celebrates its local festivals (early May and August) with a **Battle of the Moors and the Christians**, but a special event, the **Caballos del Vino**, recalls another castle-related legend. The Templar knights were under siege, but made a desperate dash to search for water. All they came up with was wine, and this event is now recalled in a procession of costumed horsemen.

Moratalla

Moratalla is a sleepy, whitewashed mountain town in the northwestern Sierras. Steep streets scramble up towards the sturdy 15th-century **castle** erected by the Knights of the Order of Santiago and the fortress-like 16th-century Iglesia de la Asunción, with spectacular views across the valley. The town celebrates some unusual festivals, including the **Fiesta del Cristo del Rayo** (Christ of Lightning) in mid-July, when heifers are let loose on the streets. It's also well known for the Tamborada, when a thousand drums are thumped ceaselessly on Maundy Thursday and Good Friday during Semana Santa.

Listings Northwest of Murcia

Where to stay

€€€-€€ Hospedería Bajo el Cejo
C/El Paso s/n, Alhama de Murcia,
T968 668 032, www.bajoelcejo.com.
A carefully renovated watermill in the Sierra Espuña, with simple yet tasteful rooms, a pool, exquisite views, and perfect tranquility.

€€ El Molino del Río
Camino Viejo de Archivel,
Caravaca de la Cruz, T968 433 381,
www.elmolinodelrio.com.
This 15th-century watermill in a beautiful rural setting 10 km from the town offers a choice of cottages and apartments in its outbuildings.

€€ Hospedería Rural Almunia
Caravaca de la Cruz, T968 730 377,
www.hotelruralmurcia.com.
Charming little hotel with individually decorated rooms in the old town, with a good café-bar downstairs.

€€ Hotel Los Bartolos
C/Alfonso X El Sabio 1, Alhama de Murcia,
T968 631 671.
A comfortable, modern option handy as a base for the Sierra de Espuña. Good mid-priced restaurant.

Transport

There are buses and trains from **Murcia** to **Alhama de Murcia** for the Sierra Espuña; an hourly bus service to **Caravaca de la Cruz** from Murcia; and at least 3 buses a day from Murcia to Moratalla.

Coastal
Murcia

The rocky coastline is pocked with quiet coves, places to relax, swim and enjoy fresh seafood. Much of the coast, particularly the Calblanque Nature Reserve, is refreshingly undeveloped with the exception of the horribly built-up La Manga and the Mar Menor. Long-neglected Cartagena is blossoming once again and has rediscovered its glorious past.

Cartagena

the lively old town is steeped in history and culture

Cartagena is one of the oldest cities on the Iberian Peninsula, set around a natural bay and scattered with monuments from several ancient civilizations. Its glory days may be over, but, after years in the doldrums as little more than a rather shabby port town, Cartagena is finally brushing itself off and has emerged as one of the most engaging little cities on the Mediterranean coast. All the sights in Cartagena are concentrated in the area around the port and are easily seen on foot.

Sights

Cartagena's old town is crowned by the **Castillo de la Concepción** ⓘ *Jul to mid-Sep daily 1000-2000, Nov-Mar Tue-Sun 1000-1730, rest of the year Tue Sun 1000-1900, €3.75/2.75, or €4.25/3.25 with lift*, which contains the remnants of an Arabic lighthouse, and is surrounded by **Parque de Torres**, pretty gardens full of strutting peacocks. Now it contains an excellent, high-tech history museum, and is reached by a panoramic glass lift, which offers spectacular views.

Below it are the impressive remnants of the **Teatro Romano (Roman theatre)** ⓘ *May-Sep Tue-Sat 1000-2000, Sun 1000-1400, Oct-Apr Tue-Sat 1000-1800, Sun 1000-1400, €6/5*, built in the first century BC and only discovered in 1987. Spanish 'starchitect' Rafael Moneo designed the sleek adjoining museum, which contains the treasures discovered during excavations, and has become one of the city's best attractions. Nearby, the **Catedral de Santa María la Vieja** ⓘ *Mon 1000-1400 and 1800-2030, Tue-Sat 1000-1400 and 1700-2030, Sun 1000-1400*, was built on top of the stalls which formed part of the theatre. There are Roman ruins scattered

BACKGROUND
Cartagena

The first settlement on this spectacular natural bay was founded by Hasdrubal Barca in 227 BC. It became a prosperous commercial port and naval base, made rich by local gold and silver mines, under the Carthaginians who named it Carthago Nova after their own capital. Later an important Roman settlement, its fortunes declined under the Visigoths and subsequent rulers – the next time Cartagena made the history books was when it was sacked by Francis Drake in 1585. In 1873, it revolted against Spain's First Republic, and was viciously bombarded as a result. Worse was to follow during the Civil War, when the city was virtually flattened. Despite this, it remains one of Spain's most important naval base, arsenal and shipyard, as well as one of its largest cruise ship ports. Its economy is further bolstered the huge energy companies which are based here, as well as the rise in tourism.

throughout the old town – you can see the remnants of a 1st-century **Roman villa**, the **Casa de la Fortuna**, or visit the **Augusteum**, where devotees of the Emperor Augustus once gathered. A stretch of the original Punic wall, built under the city's founder Hasdrubal, also survives in the **Centro de Interpretació de la Muralla Púnica** ⓘ *Jul to mid-Sep daily 1000-2000, Nov-Mar Tue-Sun 1000-1730, rest of the year Tue Sun 1000-1900, €3.50/2.50*.

The white-and-ochre-painted 18th-century **Arsenal** dominates Cartagena's port. Behind it is the **Museo Nacional de Arqueología Marítima (ARQUA)** ⓘ *C/Ramón y Cajal, T968 128 968, mid-Apr to mid-Oct Tue-Sat 1000-2100, Sun 1000-1500, mid-Oct to mid-Apr Tue-Sat 1000-2000, Sun 1000-1500 €3/1.50*, with an eclectic collection of amphorae and all kinds of bits and bobs salvaged from shipwrecks. The nearby **Museo Naval** ⓘ *C/Menéndez y Pelayo 8, T968 127 119, mid-Oct to mid-Apr Tue-Sat 1000-1330 and 1630-1900, Sun 1000-1400, mid-Apr to mid-Oct Mon-Fri 0900-1400, free*, occupies a former prison and exhibits some fascinating maps as well as replicas of ancient seacraft. The port is overlooked by a big, white torpedo, which is actually a prototype submarine designed by local engineer Isaac Peral in 1884. A string of cafés and bars now overlooks the harbour, part of the city's ongoing efforts to reinvent itself.

The **Plaza de Ayuntamiento** is overlooked by the florid Modernista **Palacio Consistorial** (which now contains the tourist office), and the **Calle Mayor**, which leads off the square has more Modernista architecture, including the prettily tiled **Casa Llagostera**, and the city **Casino**, not a place to gamble, but a cultural centre (http://casinodecartagena.org). The street comes alive in the early evening, when families come to take the *paseo*, and pause for a drink at a terrace café. The **Museo Arqueológico Municipal** ⓘ *C/Ramón y Cajal 45, T968 128 968, Tue-Fri 1000-1400 and 1700-2000, Sat-Sun 1100-1400, free*, is in the new part of town (a good 20-minute walk from the centre). It's built on top of the late Roman necropolis of San Antón, and offers an interesting introduction to Cartagena's history.

Tourist information

Cartagena Tourist Office
Palacio Consistorial, Plaza del Ayuntamiento, T968 128 955, www. cartagenaturismo.es and www. cartagenapuertodeculturas.com.

Where to stay

€€€ Hotel Cartaganova
C/Marcos Redondo 3, T968 504 200.
A modern hotel with a small spa and comfortable rooms in the old quarter.

€€ Los Habaneros
San Diego 60, T968 505 250.
Right at the entrance to the old city, with well-equipped rooms (some with jacuzzis) and a popular restaurant serving traditional cuisine.

€ Pensión-Hospedaje Oriente
C/Jara 27, T968 502 469.
Simple budget option with basic rooms in a pretty historic building, with shared bathrooms and kindly owners.

Restaurants

€€ El Barrio de San Roque
C/Jabonerías 30, T968 500 600.

An elegant restaurant in a handsomely restored warehouse, serving excellent regional dishes and great tapas prepared with originality.

€€ Mare Nostrum
Paseo de Alfonso XII, T968 522 131.
A popular, seafront seafood restaurant with a tapas bar and a terrace overlooking the port.

€€-€ La Tartana
C/Mayor 5, T968 500 011.
Enjoy tasty dishes made with local produce or tuck into the wide range tapas at the bar.

€ La Mejillonera
C/Mayor, T968 521 179.
Tuck in to the famous mussels (*mejillones*) at this cheap and cheerful tapas bar, chucking the shells into the big buckets provided.

Transport

The bus and train stations are conveniently located close to the town centre. There are regular regional and **Talgo** trains from **Murcia** to **Cartagena**, but the regional train is almost as fast and costs considerably less (about €5.25 one way as opposed to €16.80).

La Costa Cálida

some beautiful and unspoilt beaches off the beaten track

La Costa Cálida (the warm coast) lives up to its name, with average temperatures that rarely drop below 18ºC, and entices thousands of visitors every year, particularly around the Mar Menor. For wilder, emptier beaches and less built-up resorts, head down to the Golfo de Mazarrón, which is less accessible, but you might find a beach all to yourself. The most beautiful stretch of coastline – not just in Murcia, but anywhere along the Spanish Mediterranean – is preserved in the stunning Calblanque Nature Reserve.

Mar Menor and La Manga

Most of Murcia's tourist development is concentrated around the **Mar Menor**, a vast saltwater lagoon which is divided from the Mediterranean by a narrow isthmus, called **La Manga** ('the sleeve'). In the 1960s, this area was completely unspoilt, but indiscriminate building since the tourist boom began has meant that it's now clogged with unsightly development, particularly along La Manga itself. A popular package resort, the Mar Menor offers sun, sea and sand at a cheap price, with good sports facilities and spa centres.

There are several resorts around the Mar Menor. The largest are **Santiago de la Ribera** and **Los Alcázares**, where smart Murcians from the city have their summer apartments. **Lo Pagán**, at the northern end of the lagoon and surrounded by salt flats, is the least developed and most attractive. The black mud from the salt pools reputedly soothes all ailments, particularly rheumatism, and people have been coming to slather themselves for centuries. The narrow Manga is an unbroken line of grim high-rise hotels and apartment blocks, but the beaches are all long and sandy, and packed with sailing and sports facilities. Stretching west of **Cabo de Palos**, facing south, is the ★**Calblanque Nature Reserve**, a stunningly beautiful strip of unspoilt coastline, with wild beaches (and almost no facilities, so bring picnic supplies and plenty of water) backed by undulating dunes.

Golfo de Mazarrón

Southern Murcia is a dry, scrubby virtual desert – perfect tomato-growing country. The dusty land is swathed in vast tents stretching as far as the eye can see, where tomatoes are grown under ghostly plastic covers. The coastline is barely built up, except for the two modest resorts of **Aguilas** and **Puerto de Mazarrón**, and, with your own transport, it's possible to discover remote rocky coves without a soul on them. Best beaches are around the **Ciudad Encantada de Bolnuevo**, south of Mazarrón, where the rocks have been whipped into strange shapes by wind and time.

There are a couple of **tourist offices** ⓘ *Aguilas, Plaza Antonio Cortijos s/n, T968 493 173, www.aguilas.es, and at Puerto de Mazarrón, Plaza Toneleros, T968 594 426, http://visitamazarron.es.*

Listings La Costa Cálida

Transport

There are 3 bus services a day (€4) to **Los Nietos** on the **Mar Menor**. The narrow-gauge **FEVE** train also runs there every 15-30 mins. **Aguilas** and **Puerto de Mazarrón** are both reached by local buses from **Murcia** and **Cartagena**, but you'll need your own transport to find the lesser known coves.

Practicalities

Best time to visit

There's never really a bad time to visit Valencia, which enjoys year-round sunshine. If you want to bake on the beach, come any time from June to September, but to avoid the crowds, visit in late spring or late autumn. Autumn, when the rice fields around the city turn gold, is a beautiful time to visit. Las Fallas, which takes place in mid-March, is by far the city's biggest festival, so you'll need to book accommodation months in advance if you're planning to join in. In winter there are few visitors but you can still enjoy the city's wide range of cultural offerings, as well as the sunshine.

Las Fallas is not just Valencia's biggest festival but one of the biggest in Spain. Scores of smaller festivals take place through the year, including carnival, Easter, and the feast day of the Virgen de los Despamparados in May. ▸▸ *See also Festivals and public holidays, page 90.*

Getting there

Air

Spain, particularly the Mediterranean coast, is one of Europe's most popular holiday destinations, and there are hundreds of flights run by dozens of operators. This usually means a good deal for visitors, but you have to be prepared to shop around. Fares depend on the season, and the kind of ticket you buy. Ticket prices are lowest in February, November and August. One of the best ways of finding the cheapest offers is to check out flight comparison sites such as **www.skyscanner. net**, **www.momondo.com** or **www.fly.com**. Some companies regularly offer good deals which are worth looking out for, including **www.ebookers.co.uk**, **www.expedia.co.uk** and **www.lastminute.com**.

Students and those under 26 could consider booking through a specialist travel-agent such as **STA**, which has offices worldwide, **Trailfinders** in the UK, or **Council Travel** in the USA.

Rail

Travelling from the UK to Spain by train is unlikely to save either time or money, but it is a more eco-friendly way to travel and can be considerably more pleasurable. You can take the **Eurostar** ⓘ *www.eurostar.com*, *T08342-186186*, to Paris, the main rail gateway from the rest of Europe to Spain, which has high-speed and sleeper-train services to Madrid and Barcelona, with onward connections to Valencia and Murcia. For more information, contact **www.sncf.fr** (also in English), **www.raileurope.co.uk** (in the UK) or **www.rail europe.com** (in North America). Fares vary considerably, but the overnight train to Madrid costs from €400 for a return, but you'll need to book well in advance. Take a look at **www.seat61.com**, an excellent resource for European train travel.

Road

Car

The main routes into Spain are the E05/E70 motorway that runs down the southwest coast of France, crossing into Spain at Irun, near San Sebastián, and the E7, which crosses the eastern Pyrenees to Barcelona. The latter is most convenient for Valencia and Murcia. Both these motorways are fairly heavily tolled but worthwhile compared to the slow, traffic-plagued *rutas nacionales* on these sectors. Several more scenic but much slower routes cross the Pyrenees at various points. Motorways charge expensive tolls in France and Spain and ferry fares can be extremely expensive in high season. Petrol is considerably more expensive than in North America but slightly cheaper in Spain than in France and the UK. For information on driving through France, check **www.autoroute.fr** for information on motorways and traffic.

Coach

Eurolines ⓘ *52 Grosvenor Gardens, London SW1, T08717-818178, www.national express.com*, runs several buses from major European cities to a variety of destinations in Spain, including Valencia and Murcia. There are no direct services from the UK to Spain: all require a change in Paris and you will need to purchase separate tickets for each leg of the journey. Book well in advance and the entire journey could cost less than €50 (€100 return). Journey times to Valencia are between 26 and 36 hours and, unless you hate flying, air tickets will often work out cheaper.

Sea

Brittany Ferries ⓘ *T08705-360360, www.brittanyferries.co.uk*, offers a service from Plymouth to Santander, 100 km west of Bilbao, which depart up to five times a week and take about 20 hours. In Santander there's an office at the Estación Marítima (T942 360 611). Prices vary but can usually be found for about £300 for a car and two passengers. They also offer a Portsmouth to Bilbao service, which operates twice a week and takes between 24 and 32 hours.

Getting around

Rail

The Spanish national rail network, RENFE ⓘ *www.renfe.com, T902 320 320*, offers a wide variety of services, from local commuter networks (called *cercanías*) to the fast, comfortable, long-distance trains which run down the length of the Mediterranean coast.

Road

Bus

Buses are the staple of Spanish public transport. Services between major cities are fast, frequent, reliable and fairly cheap; the 4½-hour trip from Valencia to Murcia, for example, costs around €25 (one-way). **Supra** buses run on some routes; these are more expensive but luxurious and significantly faster. When buying a ticket, always check how long the journey will take, as the odd bus will be an 'all stations to' job, calling in at villages that seem surprised to even see it. Tourist offices never know how long a route takes; you must ask the bus companies themselves.

Valencia, Alicante and Murcia each have a main bus terminal, the *estación de autobuses*, which is where all short- and long-haul services leave from. Buy your tickets at the relevant window; if there isn't one, buy it from the driver. Many companies don't allow any baggage at all in the cabin of the bus, but security is pretty good. Most tickets will have a seat number (*asiento*) on them; ask when buying the ticket if you prefer a window (*de ventana*) or aisle (*de pasillo*) seat. If you're travelling at busy times (particularly a fiesta or national holiday) always book the bus ticket ahead. You can usually book tickets online with the bus company.

Rural bus services are slower, less frequent and more difficult to co-ordinate. They typically run early in the morning and late in the evening; they're designed for villagers who visit the 'big smoke' once a month or so to shop. If you're trying to catch a bus from a small stop, you'll often need to almost jump out under the wheels to get the driver to pull up. The same goes when trying to get off a bus; even if you've asked the driver to let you know when your stop comes up, keep an eye out as they tend to forget. There are hundreds of different bus companies, but most bus stations have an information window and a general enquiry line to help you out. Unfortunately, English is rarely spoken, even in the larger cities. The tourist information offices usually have timetables for bus services to tourist destinations and are a good first port-of-call before you brave the ranks of ticket windows.

All bus services are reduced on Sundays, and many on Saturdays too; some services don't run at all on weekends. Many local newspapers publish a comprehensive list of departures; expect few during siesta hours.

Car

The roads in Spain are good, excellent in many parts. While driving isn't as sedate as in parts of northern Europe, it's generally pretty good, and you'll have few problems. To drive in Spain, you'll need a full driving licence from your home country. This applies to virtually all foreign nationals, but, in practice, if you're from an 'unusual' country, consider an International Driving Licence or official translation of your licence into Spanish. Drivers are required by law to wear seatbelts and to carry two warning triangles, spares (tyres, bulbs, fanbelt) and the tools to fit them. You may also need to fit special prisms to your headlights for driving on the right if you are bringing your car from the UK or Ireland (so that they dip to the right). Front and rear seatbelts are compulsory, and children under 12 years are not permitted to ride in the front seat. Traffic circulates on the right.

There are two types of motorway in Spain, *autovías* and *autopistas*; a toll is required on an *autopista*, but otherwise they are virtually the same. The speed limit on motorways is 120 kph. On a limited number of autopistas, the speed limit has been raised to 130 kph.

Rutas nacionales form the backbone of Spain's road network. Centrally administered, they vary wildly in quality. Typically, they are choked with traffic backed up behind trucks, and there are few stretches of dual carriageway. Driving at siesta time is a good idea if you're going to be on a busy stretch. *Rutas nacionales* are marked with a red N number. The speed limit is 100 kph outside built-up areas, as it is for secondary roads, which are numbered the prefix 'C'.

In urban areas, the speed limit is 50 kph. Many towns and villages have sensors that will turn traffic lights red if you're over the limit on approach. City driving can be confusing, with signposting generally poor and traffic heavy. While not overly concerned about rural speed limits, police enforce the urban limits quite thoroughly; foreign drivers are liable to a large on-the-spot fine. Drivers can also be punished for not carrying two red warning triangles to place on the road in case of breakdown.

Parking is a problem in Valencia, as in nearly every town and city in Spain. Red or yellow lines on the side of the street mean no parking. Blue or white lines mean that some restrictions are in place; a sign will indicate what these are (typically it means that the parking is metered). Parking meters can usually only be dosed up for a maximum of two hours, but they take a siesta at lunchtime too. Print the ticket off and display it in the car. Underground parking stations are common, but fairly pricey; €15-25 is normal for 24-hour parking in big cities.

Liability insurance is required for every car driven in Spain and you must carry proof of it. If bringing your own car, check carefully with your insurers that you're covered; a green card certificate is recommended (but not obligatory). If your insurer doesn't cover you for breakdowns, consider joining the **RACE** ⓘ *T902 404 545, www.race.es*, Spain's automobile association, that provides breakdown cover.

Car hire in Spain is easy but not especially cheap. The major multinationals have offices at all large towns and airports; cheaper organizations include **ATESA** ⓘ *www.atesa.es*, which has offices at most of the larger train stations, and **Holiday Autos** ⓘ *www.holidayautos.com*. All major international car hire firms including **Avis** ⓘ *www.avis.com*; **National** ⓘ *www.nationalcar.com* (which often shares offices with **ATESA**); Hertz ⓘ *www.hertz.com*, are all represented in most cities. It's also worth checking with your airline when you book your flight if they offer any special deals on car rental. Prices start at around €250 per week for a small car with unlimited mileage. You'll need a credit card and your passport, and most agencies will either not accept under-25s or demand a surcharge.

Cycling

Cycling presents a curious contrast; Spaniards are mad for the competitive sport, but comparatively uninterested in cycling as a means of transport. Thus there are plenty of cycling shops (although beware; it can be time-consuming to find replacement parts for non-standard cycles) but very few bike lanes. However, things have changed for the better over the last few years: Valencia and Alicante operate inexpensive bike-sharing systems, and the number of bike lanes have steadily increased. Contact the **Real Federación de Ciclismo en España** ⓘ *www.rfec.com*, for more links and assistance.

Motorcycling

Motorcycling is a good way to enjoy the coast around Valencia, and there are few difficulties to trouble the biker; bike shops and mechanics are relatively common. Hiring a motorbike, however, can be difficult; most outlets are in the major cities. **Real Federación Motociclista Española** ⓘ *www.rfme.com*, can help with links and advice.

Taxi

Taxis are a convenient and reasonable option; flagfall is €2.15 in most places (it increases slightly at night), plus about €1 a kilometre. A taxi is available if its green light is lit; hail one on the street or ask for the nearest rank (*parada de taxis*).

Maps

The Michelin series of road maps are by far the most accurate for general navigation, although if you're getting off the beaten track you'll often find a local map handy. Tourist offices provide these, although they vary in quality from province to province. The **Everest** series of maps cover provinces and their main towns; they're not bad, but tend to be a bit out of date. The **Instituto Geográfico Nacional** publishes provincial maps, available at bookshops. You can order maps online in advance from the **Librería Quera** ⓘ *www.llibreriaquera.com*, or **Altair** ⓘ *www.altair.es*, both based in Spain, or from **Stanfords** ⓘ *12 Long Acre, London, WC2, T020-7836 1321, www.stanfords.co.uk*, in the UK. In the USA, **The Traveler's Choice Bookstore** ⓘ *111 Greene St, New York, T(212)941 1535*, has a good selection.

Where to stay

The standard of accommodation in Spain is reasonably high: even the most modest of *pensiones* are usually very clean and respectable. However, a great number of Spanish hotels are well-equipped but characterless places on the ugly edges of town. This guide has expressly minimized these in the listings, preferring to concentrate on more atmospheric options. When booking accommodation, be sure to check the location if that's important to you – it's easy to find yourself a 15-minute cab ride from the town you want to be in.

All registered accommodation charges a 10% value-added tax; this is often included at cheaper places and may be waived if you pay cash. If you have any problems you want to report, a last resort is to ask for the *libro de reclamaciones* (complaints book), an official document that, like stepping on cracks in the pavement, means uncertain but definitely horrible consequences for the hotel if anything is written in it.

Hoteles, hostales and pensiones

Places to stay (*alojamiento*) are divided into three main categories; the distinctions between them are in an arcane series of regulations devised by the government. *Hoteles* (marked H or HR) are graded from one to five stars and usually occupy their own building, which distinguishes them from *hostales* (Hs or HsR), which go from one to three stars. *Pensiones* (P) are the standard budget option, and are usually family-run flats in an apartment block. Although it's worth looking at a room before taking it, the majority are very acceptable. The Spanish traditions of hospitality are alive and well; even the simplest of pensiones will generally provide a towel and soap, and check-out time is almost uniformly a very civilized midday.

Paradors

Spain's famous chain of state-owned hotels, the paradors, are often set in castles, convents and other historic buildings, although there are plenty of modern ones too. Most are very luxurious, with pools, bars, fine restaurants and other fancy trimmings but standards can vary considerably. They are usually expensive, but

Price codes

Where to stay	Restaurants
€€€€ over €170	€€€ over €30
€€€ €110-170	€€ €15-30
€€ €60-110	€ under €15
€ under €60	

These price codes refer to a standard double/twin room, inclusive of the 10% IVA (value-added tax). The rates are for high season (usually Jun-Aug).

Price refers to the cost of a main course for one person, without a drink.

they offer all kinds of special deals, including a youth package, which can make them surprisingly affordable. There are about half a dozen paradors in the Valencia and Murcia area, but they are all modern. Contact one of their representatives in your own country (addresses below) or check out the website: **www.parador.es**.

Rural homes

An excellent option, if you've got transport, are the networks of rural accommodation, called a variety of things from *agroturismos* to *casas rurales*. Although these are under a different classification system, the standard is often as high as any country hotel. The best of them are traditional farmhouses or old village cottages. Some are available to rent out whole, while others operate more or less as guesthouses. Rates tend to be excellent compared to hotels. Each regional government publishes their own listings booklet, which is available at any tourist office in the area, or you could check out websites such as **www.casarural.co.uk**.

Albergues and refugios

There are a few youth hostels (*albergues*) around, but the price of *pensiones* rarely makes it worth the trouble except for solo travellers. Spanish youth hostels are frequently populated by schoolkids, and have curfews and check-out times unsuitable for the late hours the locals keep. The exception is in mountain regions, where there are *refugios*: simple hostels for walkers and climbers along the lines of a Scottish bothy. Some official youth hostels require an international youth hostel card, available in advance from the international youth hostel associations.

Campsites

Most campsites are set up as well-equipped holiday villages for families; many are open only in summer. While the facilities are good, they get extremely busy in peak season; the social scene is good, but sleep can be tough. In other areas, camping, unless specifically prohibited, is a matter of common sense: most locals will know of (or offer) a place where you can pitch a tent *tranquilamente*.

Food and drink

Spaniards eat very little for breakfast, usually just a coffee and maybe a croissant or pastry. Some might tuck into *chocolate y churros* – thick, sticky hot chocolate with thin doughnut-like batter strips. They may have a quick bite and a drink in a café or bar before lunch, which is usually eaten between 1400 and 1530 or thereabouts. This is the main meal of the day and the cheapest time to eat, as most restaurants offer a cheap set menu (*menú del día*). Lunch (and dinner) is much extended at weekends, particularly on Sundays, when it seems to go on until the football kicks off in the evening. It's common to have an evening drink or tapa in a bar after the *paseo*; if this is extended into a food crawl it's called a *tapeo*. Dinner (*cena*) is normally eaten from about 2200 onwards, although sitting down to dinner at midnight at weekends isn't unusual. In smaller towns and midweek you might not get fed after 2230, so beware. Most restaurants are closed Sunday nights, and usually take a day off, either Monday or Tuesday.

Food

While the regional differences in the cuisine of Spain are important, the basics remain the same. Spanish cooking relies on meat, fish/seafood, beans and potatoes given character by the chef's holy trinity: garlic, peppers and, of course, olive oil. The influence of the colonization of the Americas is evident, and the Moors left a lasting culinary legacy, particularly in the south. The result is a hearty, filling style of meal ideally washed down with some of the nation's excellent wines.

Fish and seafood Even in areas far from the coast, the availability of good fish and seafood can be taken for granted. *Merluza* (hake) and *bacalao* (salt cod) are the staple fish, while *gambas* (prawns) are another common and excellent choice. Calamari, squid and cuttlefish are common; if you can cope with the slightly slimy texture, *pulpo* (octopus) is particularly good, especially when simply boiled *a la gallega* (Galician style) and flavoured with paprika and olive oil. Supreme among the finny tribe are *rodaballo* (turbot, best wild or *salvaje*) and *rape* (monkfish).

Meat Wherever you go, you'll find cured ham (*jamón serrano*), which is always excellent, but particularly so if it's the pricey *ibérico*, taken from acorn-eating porkers in Extremadura. Other cold meats to look out for are *cecina*, made from beef, and, of course, cured sausages (*embutidos*), including the versatile chorizo.

Pork is also popular as a cooked meat; its most common form is sliced loin (*lomo*). In mountainous regions, you'll find roast sucking pig (*cochinillo* or *lechón*), ideal for keeping out the winter cold. *Lechazo* is the lamb equivalent. Beef is common; cheaper cuts predominate, but the better steaks (*solomillo*, *chuletón*) are usually superbly tender. Spaniards tend to eat them rare (*poco hecho*; ask for *a punto* for medium or *bien hecho* for well done). The *chuletón* is worth a mention in its own right; a massive T-bone best taken from an ox (*de buey*) and sold by weight, which often approaches a kilogram. It's an imposing slab of meat indeed.

RECIPE
A taste for tortilla

Tortilla is perhaps the classic dish of Spain. Served everywhere and eaten at virtually every time of the day, it is easy to prepare and can be eaten either hot or cold. Typically served as tapas or with a salad its key features are the layering of the potatoes and its rounded shape, enabling it to be eaten in slices.

Method (serves 6)
1 large frying pan for potatoes
1 small, fairly deep frying pan
6 fresh eggs
750 g of potatoes
half a medium onion (if desired)
enough good quality olive oil to cover the potatoes in a frying pan
salt

Total cooking and preparation time around 1 hour.

Wash and peel the potatoes then slice thinly so they are about 0.5 cm in thickness. Place them in a mixing bowl and sprinkle with salt ensuring that each piece is coated with a little salt. Cut and slice the onion into small pieces about 2 cm long and add to the potatoes.

Place the salted potatoes and onions in a large frying pan and pour in enough olive oil nearly to cover them. It is essential to use good quality oil – Spanish cooks would never dream of using inferior oil for tortilla. Keep the pan at a low heat and continue to stir the potatoes regularly to ensure they do not burn or become crisp. Remove the cooked potatoes and onion from the pan and drain the oil. Total cooking time should be between 15-20 minutes depending on the thickness of the potatoes.

Mix the eggs in a mixing bowl. It is not necessary to add salt as the potatoes should have enough seasoning. Milk and pepper are rarely used in Spanish cooking but will not radically affect the taste if preferred. Prepare a new smaller pan which is deep enough to contain the egg mix and the potatoes. Place the cooked and drained potatoes in first and then add the egg mix. Fry the mixture, keeping the heat very low. When the mixture is showing signs of becoming solid remove the pan from the heat and find a plate large enough to cover the pan.

The next stage is the only tricky bit as the mixture now has to be turned over to cook the other side. Turn the solid mix on to the plate and then return it to the pan ensuring the uncooked side is facing the bottom of the pan. Continue to cook until the tortilla is solid. Total frying time should be around 10 minutes. Remove the tortilla from the pan and eat either hot or leave to cool and eat later.

Pollo (chicken) is common, but usually unremarkable; game birds such as *codorniz* (quail) and *perdiz* (partridge) are also widely eaten. The innards of animals are popular in Madrid, but less so along the Mediterranean coast. Still, you'll find *callos* (tripe), *mollejas* (sweetbreads) and *morcilla* (black pudding in solid or liquid form) on the menu. Fans of the unusual will be keen to try *jabalí* (wild boar), *potro* (horse) and *oreja* (ear, usually from a pig or sheep).

Vegetable dishes and accompaniments Main dishes often come without any accompaniments, or chips at best. The consolation, however, is the *ensalada mixta*, whose simple name (mixed salad) can often conceal a meal in itself. The ingredients vary, but it's typically a plentiful combination of lettuce, tomato, onion, olive oil, boiled eggs, asparagus, olives and tuna. The *tortilla*, see box, opposite, is ever-present and often excellent. Another common dish is *revuelto* (scrambled eggs), usually tastily combined with prawns, asparagus or other goodies.

Most vegetable dishes are based around that American trio, the bean, the pepper, and the potato. There are numerous varieties of beans in Spain; they are normally served as some sort of hearty stew, often with bits of meat or seafood to avoid the accusation of vegetarianism. *Fabada* is the Asturian classic of this variety, while *alubias con chorizo* are a standard across the northern Spain. The Catalan version is *faves a la catalana*, broad beans cooked with ham. A *cocido* is a typical mountain dish from the centre of Spain, a massive stew of chickpeas or beans with meat and vegetables. Peppers (*pimientos*), too, come in a confusing number of forms. As well as being used to flavour dishes, they are often eaten in their own right; *pimientos rellenos* come stuffed with meat and seafood. Potatoes come as chips, *bravas* (with a garlic or spicy tomato sauce) or, more interestingly, *a la riojana*, with chorizo and paprika. Other common vegetable dishes include *menestra* (think of a good minestrone soup with the liquid drained off), which usually has some ham in it, and *ensaladilla rusa*, a tasty blend of potato, peas, peppers, carrots and mayonnaise. *Setas* (wild mushrooms) are a particular delight, especially in autumn, but they are rarely found in the south.

Desserts and cheeses Desserts focus on the sweet and milky. *Flan* (a sort of crème caramel) is ubiquitous; great when *casero* (home-made), but often out of a plastic tub. *Natillas* are a similar but more liquid version, and *arroz con leche* is a cold, sweet rice pudding.

Cheeses tend to be bland or salty and are normally eaten as a tapa or entrée. There are some excellent cheeses in Spain, however; the most famous is the dry, pungent Manchego, a cured sheep's milk cheese from La Mancha, but piquant Cabrales and Basque Idiázabal also stand out.

Regional cuisine
Regional styles tend to use the same basic ingredients treated in slightly different ways, backed up by some local specialities. Food-producing regions take their responsibilities seriously, and competition is fierce. Those widely acknowledged to produce the best will often add the name of the region to the foodstuff (some

foods, like wines, have denomination of origin status given by a regulatory body). Thus *pimientos de Padrón* (Padrón peppers), *cogollos de Tudela* (lettuce hearts from Tudela), *alubias de Tolosa* (Tolosa beans) and a host of others.

Most of Spain grudgingly concedes that Basque cuisine is the peninsula's best, the San Sebastián twilight shimmers with Michelin stars, and chummy all-male *txokos* gather in private to swap recipes and cook up feasts in members-only kitchens. But what strikes the visitor first are the *pintxos*, a stunning range of bartop snacks that in many cases seem too pretty to eat. The base of most Basque dishes is seafood, particularly *bacalao* (salt cod; occasionally stunning but often humdrum), and the region has taken full advantage of its French ties.

Navarran and Aragonese cuisine owes much to the mountains, with hearty stews and game dishes featuring alongside fresh trout. Rioja and Castilla y León go for filling roast meat and bean dishes more suited to the harsh winters than the baking summers. Asturias and Cantabria are seafood-minded on the coast but search for more warming fare in the high ground, and Galicia is seafood heaven, with more varieties of finny and shelly things than you knew there were; usually prepared with confidence in the natural flavours, whereas the rest of the area overuses garlic to eliminate any fishy taste.

The Catalans are almost as famous for their cuisine as the Basques. Seafood from the Mediterranean, rice and vegetables from the plains and meat and game from the mountains are combined in unusual ways; look out for *mandonguilles amb sèpia*, meatballs with cuttlefish, or *gambas con pollastre*, prawns with chicken. The local staple is *pa amb tomàquet*, country bread rubbed with fresh tomatoes, with a little oil and salt. Valencia is famous as the birthplace of paella, a surprisingly difficult dish that is often made badly elsewhere in Spain, much to the annoyance of Valencianos. The genuine article is made with starchy *bomba* rice grown in the Valencian plains, and real saffron (not yellow food colouring, which is common), which is simmered in a shallow pan with garlic and olive oil, and a mixture of meat and/or seafood (depending on the recipe – no one can agree on the ingredients of the definitive paella). The finishing touch is the *soccarat*, a crunchy crust formed by turning up the heat for a few minutes just before the paella is cooked.

Typical Madrileño cuisine reflects the city's land-locked status in the middle of a vast plain; hunks of roast meats and hearty stews, like *cocido*, a thick broth of chickpeas, vegetables and hunks of meat, which are cooked together and served in separate courses – often over several days. Spaniards in general, and Madrileños in particular, don't turn their noses up at any part of an animal, and another local speciality is *callos a la madrileño*, a tripe dish cooked in a spicy tomato sauce. It's not unusual to find *orejas* (pigs' ears), *sesos* (brains), *riñones* (kidneys) and even *criadillas* (bulls' testicles) on the menu. If you head out to Segovia, be sure to try *cochinillo*, roast suckling pig, traditionally slaughtered when they are 21 days old. Ideally, it should be tender enough to cut with a butter knife.

In Andalucía, the Moorish inheritance is felt most strongly. The Arabs cultivated olives, saffron and almonds, which all appear in the local cuisine. There's plenty of fresh seafood along the coast and *pescadito frito*, fried fresh fish best eaten out of a paper cone, is the specialitiy of Cádiz. Inland the emphasis is on meat and game:

one of the region's best known dishes is *rabo de toro* – bull's tail slowly cooked in a rich sauce. You might already have tried gazpacho – a cold soup of tomatoes, onions and cucumber – but there's a delicious thicker version called *salmorejo*, usually topped with chopped ham and boiled eggs, and a white soup called *ajo blanco* in which the tomatoes have been replaced with almonds.

Extremadura is known for its *migas*, breadcrumbs fried with peppers, but it's most famous culinary export is the *jamón ibérico*. This is the king of hams – and Spain has countless varieties – and is made from the flesh of the *pata negra* (black foot) pigs which roam the Extremaduran *dehesa* and are fed on acorns. Watch out, though, if you order it in a tapas bar; it's very, very expensive.

Restaurants in Valencia and Costa Blanca → *See box, page 79, for price code information.*
One of the great pleasures of travelling in Spain is eating out, but it's no fun sitting alone in a restaurant so try and adapt to the local hours as much as you can; it may feel strange leaving dinner until after 2200, but you'll miss out on a lot of atmosphere if you don't.

The standard distinctions of bar, café and restaurant don't apply in Spain. Many places combine all three functions, and it's not always evident; the dining room (*comedor*) is often tucked away behind the bar or upstairs. *Restaurantes* are restaurants, and will usually have a dedicated dining area with set menus and à la carte options. Bars and cafés will often display food on the counter, or have a list of tapas; bars tend to be known for particular dishes they do well. Many bars, cafés and restaurants don't serve food on Sunday nights, and most are closed one other night a week, most commonly Monday.

Cafés will normally have some breakfasty fare out in the mornings; croissants and sweetish pastries are the norm; fresh squeezed orange juice is also common. About 1100 they start putting out savoury fare; maybe a tortilla, some *ensaladilla rusa*, or little ham rolls in preparation for pre-lunch snacking.

Lunch is the biggest meal of the day for most people in Spain, and it's also the cheapest time to eat. Just about all restaurants offer a *menú del día*, which is usually a set three-course meal that includes wine or soft drink. In unglamorous workers' locals this is often as little as €7 or €8; paying anything more than €15 indicates the restaurant takes itself quite seriously. There's often a choice of several starters and mains. To make the most of the meal, a handy tip is to order another starter in place of a main; most places are quite happy to do it, and the starters are usually more interesting (and sometimes larger) than the mains, which tend to be slabs of mediocre meat. Most places open for lunch at about 1300, and stop serving at 1500 or 1530, although at weekends this can extend; it's not uncommon to see people still lunching at 1800 on a Sunday. The quality of à la carte is usually higher than the *menú*, and quantities are large. Simpler restaurants won't offer this option except in the evenings.

Tapas has changed in meaning over the years, and now basically refers to all bar food. Prices of tapas basically depend on the ingredients; a good portion of *langostinos* (king prawns) will likely set you back €12 or 15, while more *morcilla* (black pudding) or *patatas* than you can eat might only be €5 or so.

Most restaurants open for dinner at 2030 or later; any earlier and it's likely a tourist trap. Although some places do offer a cheap set menu, you'll usually have to order à la carte. In quiet areas, places stop serving at 2200 on weeknights, but in cities and at weekends people tend to sit down at 2230 or later.

A cheap option at any time of day is a *plato combinado*, most commonly done in cafés. They're usually a truckstop-style combination of eggs, steak, bacon and chips or similar and are filling but rarely inspiring.

Vegetarians in Spain won't be spoiled for choice, but at least what there is tends to be good. Dedicated vegetarian restaurants are amazingly few, and most restaurants won't have a vegetarian main course on offer, although the existence of *raciones* and salads makes this less of a burden than it might be. *Ensalada mixta* nearly always has tuna in it, but it's usually made fresh, so places will happily leave it out. *Ensaladilla rusa* is normally a good option, but ask about the tuna too, just in case. Tortilla is another simple but nearly ubiquitous option. Simple potato or pepper dishes are tasty options (although beware peppers stuffed with meat), and many *revueltos* (scrambled eggs) are just mixed with asparagus. Annoyingly, most vegetable *menestras* are seeded with ham before cooking, and bean dishes usually have at least some meat or animal fat. You'll have to specify *soy vegetariano/a* (I am a vegetarian), but ask what dishes contain, as ham, fish, and even chicken are often considered suitable vegetarian fare. Vegans will have a tougher time. What doesn't have meat nearly always has cheese or egg, and waiters are unlikely to know the ingredients down to the basics.

Drink

Wine In good Catholic fashion, wine is the blood of Spain. It's the standard accompaniment to most meals, but also features prominently in bars, where a glass of cheap *tinto* or *blanco* can cost as little as €1, although it's normally more. A bottle of house wine in a restaurant is often no more than €8 or €9. *Tinto* is red (although if you just order *vino* it's assumed that's what you want) *blanco* is white, and rosé is either *clarete* or *rosado*.

A well-regulated system of *denominaciones de origen* (DO), similar to the French *appelation controlée*, has lifted the reputation of Spanish wines high above the party plonk status they once enjoyed. Much of Spain's wine is produced in the north, and recent years have seen regions such as the Ribera del Duero, Rueda, Navarra, Penedès and Rías Baixas achieve worldwide recognition. But the daddy is, of course, still Rioja.

The overall standard of Riojas has improved markedly since the granting of the higher DOC status in 1991, with some fairly stringent testing in place. Red predominates; these are mostly medium-bodied bottles from the Tempranillo grape (with three other permitted red grapes often used to add depth or character). Whites from Viura and Malvasia are also produced: the majority of these are young, fresh and dry, unlike the powerful oaky Rioja whites sold in the UK. Rosés are also produced. The quality of individual Riojas varies widely according to both producer and the amount of time the wines have been aged in oak barrels and in the bottle. The words *crianza*, *reserva*, and *gran reserva* refer to the length of the aging process, while the vintage date is also given. Rioja producers store their wines at the bodega until deemed ready for drinking, so it's common to see wines dating back a decade or more on shelves and wine lists.

A growing number of people feel, however, that Spain's best reds come from further west, in the Ribera del Duero region east of Valladolid. The king's favourite tipple, Vega Sicilia, has long been Spain's most prestigious wine, but other producers from the area have also gained stellar reviews. The region has been dubbed 'the Spanish Burgundy'; the description isn't wholly fanciful, as the better wines have the rich nose and dark delicacy vaguely reminiscent of the French region.

Galicia produces some excellent whites too; the coastal Albariño vineyards produce a sought-after dry wine with a very distinctive bouquet. Ribeiro is another good Galician white, and the reds from there are also tasty, having some similarity to those produced in nearby northern Portugal.

Among other regions, Navarra, long known only for rosé, is producing some quality red wines unfettered by the stricter rules governing production in neighbouring Rioja, while Bierzo, in western León province, also produces interesting wines from the red Prieto Picudo grape. Other DO wines in Northern Spain include Somontano, a red and white appelation from Aragón and Toro, whose baking climate makes for full-bodied reds.

An unusual wine worth trying is *txakolí*, with a small production on the Basque coast. The most common form is a young, refreshing, acidic white which has a green tinge and a slight sparkle, often accentuated by pouring from a height. The best examples, from around Getaria, go beautifully with seafood. The wine is made from underripe grapes of the Ondarrubi Zuria variety; there's a less common red species and some rosé.

Catalan wines are also gaining increasing recognition. Best known is cava, the home-grown bubbly, and a night out in Barcelona should always start with a glass or two of this crisp, sparkling white wine. The largest wine-producing region in Catalunya is Penedès, which produces a vast range of reds, whites and rosés to suit all tastes and pockets, but you'll find other local specialities including the unusual Paxarete, a very sweet traditional chocolatey brown wine produced around Tarragona.

One of the joys of Spain, though, is the rest of the wine. Order a *menú del día* at a cheap restaurant and you'll be unceremoniously served a cheap bottle of local red (sometimes without even asking for it). Wine snobbery can leave by the back door at this point: it may be cold, but you'll find it refreshing; it may be acidic, but once the olive-oil laden food arrives, you'll be glad of it. Wine's not a luxury item in Spain, so people add water to it if they feel like it, or lemonade, or cola (to make the party drink called *calimocho*).

In many bars, you can order Ribera, Rueda, or other regions by the glass. If you simply ask for *crianza* or *reserva*, you'll usually get a Rioja. A *tinto* or *blanco* will get you the house wine (although many bartenders in tourist areas assume that visitors don't want it, and will try and serve you a more expensive kind). As a general rule, only bars that serve food serve wine; most pubs and *discotecas* won't have it.

Beer Spanish beer is mostly lager, usually reasonably strong, fairly gassy, cold, and good. On the tapas trail, many people order *cortos*, usually about 100 ml. A *caña* is a larger draught beer, usually about 200-300 ml. Order a *cerveza* and you'll get a bottled beer. Many people order their beer con gas, topped up with mineral water, sometimes called a *clara*, although this normally means it's topped with lemonade. A *jarra* is a shared jug.

Cider Sidra is an institution in Asturias, and to a lesser extent in Euskadi, but you'll find it in Basque and Asturian restaurants in most of the larger cities. The cider is flat, sourish, and yeasty; the appley taste will be a surprise after most commercial versions of the drink.

Sherry If you thought sherry was for old ladies and vicars, think again. At Sevilla's famous Feria, the standard tipple is a glass of refreshing chilled *manzanilla*, a pale, dry and delicious thirst-quencher. There are dozens of other varieties including the light *fino* which is drunk young, or sweeter *amontillados* with a caramel flavour. The very sweetest are *olorosos*, a traditional dessert accompaniment.

Spirits *Vermut* (vermouth) is a popular pre-dinner aperitif, usually served straight from the barrel. Many bars make their own vermouth by adding various herbs and fruits and letting it sit in barrels: this can be excellent, particularly if it's from a *solera*. This is a system where liquid is drawn from the oldest of a series of barrels, which is then topped up with the next oldest, etc, resulting in some very mellow characterful drink.

After dinner people relax over a whisky or a brandy, or hit the mixed drinks: gin tonic is obvious, while a *cuba libre* is a rum and coke (but can refer to vodka or other spirits). Spirits are free-poured and large; don't be surprised at a 100 ml measure. Whisky is popular, and most bars have a good range. Spanish brandy is good, although it's oaky vanilla flavours don't appeal to everyone. There are numerous varieties of rum and flavoured liqueurs. When ordering a spirit, you'll be expected to choose which brand you want; the local varieties (eg Larios gin, DYC whisky) are marginally cheaper than their imported brethren. *Chupitos* are shots; restaurants will often throw in a free one at the end of a meal, or give you a bottle of *orujo* (grape spirit) to pep up your black coffee.

Non-alcoholic drinks Juice is normally bottled and expensive, although freshly squeezed orange juice is common. It's an odd thing to order after breakfast, though. *Mosto* (grape juice; really pre-fermented wine) is a cheaper and popular soft drink in bars. There's the usual range of fizzy drinks (*gaseosas*) available, but a popular and peculiarly Spanish soft drink is **Bitter-kas**, a dark red herby brew which tastes a bit like Campari. *Horchata* is a summer drink, a sort of milkshake made from tiger nuts which comes from the Valencia region but is popular throughout Spain. Water (*agua*) comes *con* (with) or *sin* (without) gas. The tap water is totally safe to drink, but it's not always the best tasting.

Hot drinks Coffee (*café*) is usually excellent and strong. *Solo* is black, mostly served espresso style. Order *americano* if you want it long and black, *cortado* if you want a dash of milk, or *con leche* for about half milk. A *carajillo* is a coffee with brandy, while *queimado* is a coffee heated with *orujo*. *Té* (tea) is served without milk unless you ask; herbal teas (*infusiones*) can be found in many places. Chocolate is a reasonably popular drink at breakfast time or as a *merienda* (afternoon tea), served with *churros*, fried doughsticks that seduce about a quarter of visitors and repel the rest.

Essentials A-Z

Accident and emergencies

There is now one nationwide emergency number for fire, police and ambulance: T112.

Electricity

The current in Spain is 220V. A round 2-pin plug is used (European standard).

Embassies and consulates

For embassies and consulates of Spain abroad, see http://embassy.goabroad.com.

Festivals and public holidays

Even the smallest village in Spain has a fiesta, and some have several. Although mostly nominally religious in nature, they usually include the works; a Mass and procession or 2 to be sure, but also live music, bullfights, competitions, fireworks and copious drinking of *calimocho*, a mix of red wine and cola (not as bad as it sounds). A feature of many are the *gigantes y cabezudos*, huge-headed papier-mâché figures based on historical personages who parade the streets. Adding to the sense of fun are *peñas*, boisterous social clubs which patrol the streets making music, get rowdy at the bullfights and drink wine all night and day. Most fiestas are in summer, and if you're spending much time in Spain in that period you're bound to run into one; expect some trouble finding accommodation. Details of the major town fiestas can be found throughout the book. National holidays can be

difficult times to travel; it's important to reserve tickets in advance. If the holiday falls mid-week, it's usual form to take an extra day off, creating a long weekend known as a *puente* (bridge).

Major fiestas

5 Jan Cabalgata de Los Reyes (Three Kings). Throughout Spain. The Three Kings Parade in floats tossing out sweets to kids, who get Christmas presents the next day.

Feb/Mar Carnaval. Held in almost every town and village.

Mid-Mar Las Fallas. Valencia sees massive street parades and the burning of huge papier-mâché creations. See box, page 18.

Easter Semana Santa. Easter celebrations are held everywhere and parades take place in every town, particularly in the south of Spain.

End May/Jun Feast of Corpus Christi. Held in most towns, it is celebrated with traditional dancing and parades.

21-24 Jun Fiesta de San Juan, or the Midsummer's Solstice. This is celebrated across Spain, often with bullfights, or with the strange custom of the 'Burial of the Sardine'.

Aug Mystery plays. Performed in the baroque cathedral in Elche.

La Tomatina, in Buñol, see box, page 41.

Public holidays

1 Jan Año Nuevo (New Year's Day)
6 Jan Reyes Magos (Epiphany) when Christmas presents are given.

Easter **Jueves Santo**, **Viernes Santo**, **Día de Pascua** (Maundy Thu, Good Fri, Easter Sun).
1 May **Fiesta de Trabajo** (Labour Day).
15 Aug **Asunción** (Feast of the Assumption).
12 Oct **Día de la Hispanidad** (Columbus Day, Spanish National Day, Feast of the Virgin of the Pillar).
1 Nov **Todos los Santos** (All Saints' Day).
6 Dec **Día de la Constitución Española** (Constitution Day).
8 Dec **Inmaculada Concepción** (Feast of the Immaculate Conception).
24 Dec **Noche Buena** (Christmas Eve).
25 Dec **Navidad** (Christmas Day).

Health

Health for travellers in Spain is rarely a problem. Medical facilities are good, and the worst most travellers experience is an upset stomach, usually merely a result of the different diet rather than any bug. The water is safe to drink, but doesn't always taste great, so many travellers (and locals) stick to bottled water. The sun can be harsh, so take precautions to avoid heat exhaustion/sunburn. Many medications that require a prescription in other countries are available over the counter at pharmacies in Spain. Pharmacists are highly trained but don't necessarily speak English. In all medium-sized towns and cities, at least one pharmacy is open 24 hrs; this is organized on a rota system; details are posted in the window of all pharmacies and listed in local newspapers.

Hospitals
Hospital Clínico, Av de Blasco Ibáñez 17, Valencia, T963 862 600.

Insurance

British and other European citizens should obtain a European Health Insurance Card (EHIC) available via www.dh.gov.uk or from post offices in the UK, before leaving home. This guarantees free medical care throughout the EU. Non-EU citizens should consider insurance to cover emergency and routine medical needs; be sure that it covers any sports/activities you may get involved in.

Insurance is a good idea anyway to cover you for theft, etc. Any theft must be reported at the local police station within 24 hrs; you'll need to obtain a written report to show your insurers.

Language

→ *See page 96 for some useful words and phrases.*
For travelling purposes, everyone in Spain speaks Spanish, known either as *castellano* or *español*. Most young people know some English, and standards are rising, but don't assume that people aged 30 or over know any at all. While efforts to speak the language are appreciated, it's more or less expected, to the same degree as English is expected in Britain or the USA. Nobody will be rude if you don't speak any Spanish, but nobody will think to slow down their speech for your benefit either. While many visitor attractions have information available in English (and sometimes French and German), many don't, or only have English tours in times of high demand. Most tourist office staff will speak at least some English, and there's a good range of translated information available in many regions.

Valenciano is widely spoken in the inland regions of Valencia, although markedly less so along the coast. In the Valencian capital, they regularly combine *castellano* and *valenciano* in the same phrase or street name with a blithe disregard for linguistic purity. Any efforts to speak the local language – even a simple *bon dia* instead of *hola* or 'hello' – will be very much appreciated.

Money

Currency

See www.xe.com for exchange rates. The euro (€) is divided into 100 céntimos. Euro notes are standard across the whole zone, and come in denominations of 5, 10, 20, 50, 100, and the rarely seen 200 and 500. Coins have one standard face and one national face; all coins are, however, acceptable in all countries. The coins are slightly difficult to tell apart when you're not used to them. The coppers are 1, 2 and 5 cent pieces, the golds are 10, 20 and 50, and the silver/gold combinations are €1 and €2.

ATMs and banks

The best way to get money in Spain is by plastic. ATMs are plentiful, and just about all of them accept all the major international debit and credit cards. The Spanish bank won't charge for the transaction, though they will charge a mark-up on the exchange rate, but beware of your own bank hitting you for a hefty fee: check with them before leaving home. Even if they do, it's likely to be a better deal than exchanging cash. The website www.moneysavingexpert.com has a good rundown on the most economical ways of accessing cash while travelling.

Banks are usually open Mon-Fri 0830-1400 (and Sat in winter) and many change foreign money (sometimes only the central branch in a town will do it). Commission rates vary widely; it's usually best to change large amounts, as there's often a minimum commission of €6 or so. Nevertheless, banks nearly always give better rates than change offices (*casas de cambio*), which are fewer by the day. If you're stuck outside banking hours, some large department stores such as **El Corte Inglés** change money at knavish rates.

Traveller's cheques are still accepted in many shops, although they are far less common than they were. You may find that a pre-paid currency card, issued in the UK by the post office or by specialist money-changing companies, such as **Travelex** and **Caxton FX**, are more useful.

Tax

Nearly all goods and services in Spain are subject to a value-added tax (IVA). This is currently 10% for most things the traveller will encounter, including restaurants and hotels, but is as high as 21% on some things. IVA is normally included in the stated prices. You're technically entitled to claim it back if you're a non-EU citizen, for purchases over €90. If you're buying something pricey, make sure you get a stamped receipt clearly showing the IVA component, as well as your name and passport number; you can claim the amount back at major airports on departure. Some shops will have a form to smooth the process.

Cost of living and travelling

Spain can still be a reasonably cheap place to travel if you're prepared to forgo a few luxuries. If you're travelling as a pair, staying in cheap *pensiones*, eating a set meal at lunchtime, travelling short distances by bus or train daily, and snacking on tapas in the evenings, €70 per person per day is reasonable. If you camp and grab picnic lunches from shops, you could reduce this considerably. In a cheap hotel or good hostal and using a car, €130 a day and you'll not be counting pennies; €250 per day and you'll be very comfy indeed unless you're staying in 4- or 5-star accommodation.

Accommodation is more expensive in summer than in winter. The news isn't great for the solo traveller; single rooms tend not to be particularly good value, and they are in short supply. Prices range from 60-80% of the double/twin price; some places even charge the full rate. If you're going to be staying in 3- to 5-star hotels, booking them ahead on internet discount sites, such as www.booking. com or www.budgetplaces.com, can save a lot of money.

Public transport is generally cheap; intercity bus services are quick and low-priced and trains are reasonable, though the fast AVE trains cost substantially more.

Petrol is relatively cheap: standard unleaded petrol is around €1.38 per litre and diesel around €1.35. In some places, particularly in tourist areas, you may be charged up to 20% more to sit outside a restaurant. It's also worth checking if the 10% IVA (sales tax) is included in menu prices, especially in the more expensive restaurants; it should say on the menu whether this is the case.

Opening hours

Offices are usually open Mon-Fri 0800-1500. These hours might be official, but time in Spain is always fluid.

Safety

Spain is generally a safe place, with considerably less violent crime than many other European countries. However, street crime – bag-snatching and pickpocketing – in the bigger cities is on the rise. Don't invite crime by leaving luggage or cash in cars, and if you are parking in a city or a popular hiking zone, leave the glove box open so that thieves know there is nothing to steal.

There are several types of police, helpful enough in normal circumstances. The paramilitary Guardia Civil dress in green and are responsible for the roads (including speed traps and the like), borders and law enforcement away from towns. They're not a bunch to get the wrong side of but are polite to tourists and have thankfully lost the bizarre winged hats they used to sport. The Policía Nacional are responsible for most urban crimefighting. These are the ones to go to if you need to report anything stolen, etc. Policía Local/Municipal are present in large towns and cities and are responsible for some urban crime, as well as traffic control and parking. Police stations are listed in phone books under *comisarías*. See also Insurance, page 91.

Telephone → *Country code +34.*

There are very few public telephones on the streets nowadays, and those that exist generally take credit cards or pre-paid phone cards, which can be bought from tobacconists (*estancos*) in denominations of €5, €10 or €20. Few accept coins. Calls are cheaper after 2200 during the week and all day at weekends. Phones in bars and cafés usually have more expensive rates than public payphones. Phone centres (*locutarios*) are the cheapest method for calling abroad.

For directory enquiries, dial T11818 for national or T11825 for international numbers. (All these numbers are operated by **Telefónica**; other operators offer the same services).

Domestic landlines have 9-digit numbers beginning with 9 (occasionally with 8). Although the 1st 3 digits indicate the province, you have to dial the full number from wherever you are calling, including abroad. Mobile numbers start with 6.

Mobile (*móviles*) coverage is very good. Most foreign mobiles will work in Spain; check with your service provider about what the call costs will be like. Many mobile networks require you to call up before leaving your home country to activate overseas service ('roaming'). If you're staying a while, it may be cheaper to buy a Spanish mobile or SIM card, as there are always numerous offers and discounts.

Time

Spain operates on western European time, ie GMT +1, and changes its clocks in line with the rest of the EU.

'Spanish time' isn't as elastic as it used to be, but if you're told something will happen *'en seguida'* ('straight away') it may take 10 mins, if you're told *'cinco minutos'* (5 mins), grab a seat and a book. Transport, especially buses, leaves promptly.

Tipping

Tipping in Spain is far from compulsory, but much practised. Around 10% is considered fairly generous in a restaurant; 3-5% is more usual. It's rare for a service charge to be added to a bill. Waiters do not normally expect tips for lunchtime set meals or tapas, but here and in bars and cafés people will often leave small change, especially for table service. Taxi drivers don't expect a tip, but don't expect you to sit around waiting for 20 cents change either. In rural areas, churches will often have a local keyholder who will open it up for you; if there's no admission charge, a tip or donation is appropriate; say €1 per head; more if they've given a detailed tour.

Toilets

Public toilets are not common, although you'll find them in train stations. It's usually okay to use the ones in bars and cafés. You might have to use the bin next to the loo for your toilet paper if the system can't cope, particularly in out-of-the-way places. There are usually toilets in the big department stores, too.

Tourist information

The tourist information infrastructure in Spain is organized by the regional governments and is generally excellent, with a wide range of information, often in English, German and French as well as Spanish. Offices within the region can provide maps of the area and towns, and lists of registered accommodation, usually with a booklet for hotels, *hostales*, and *pensiones*; another for campsites, and another, especially worth picking up, listing farmstay and rural accommodation, which has taken off in a big way; hundreds are added yearly. Opening hours are longer in major cities; many rural offices are only open in summer. Average opening hours are Mon-Sat 1000-1400, 1600-1900, Sun 1000-1400. Offices are often closed on Sun or Mon. Staff often speak English and other European languages.

Visas and immigration

Entry requirements are subject to change, so always check with the Spanish tourist board or an embassy/consulate.if you're not an EU citizen. EU citizens and those from countries within the Schengen agreement can enter Spain freely. UK/Irish citizens will need to carry a passport, while an identity card suffices for other EU/Schengen nationals. Citizens of Australia, the USA, Canada, New Zealand and Israel can enter without a visa for up to 90 days. Other citizens will require a visa, obtainable from Spanish consulates or embassies. These are usually issued very quickly and valid for all Schengen countries. The basic visa is valid for 90 days, and you'll need 2 passport photos, proof of funds covering your stay, and possibly evidence of medical cover (ie insurance). For extensions of visas, apply to an *oficina de extranjeros* in a major city.

Weights and measures

The Spanish use the metric system. Decimal places are indicated with commas, and thousands with points.

Spanish words & phrases

Greetings, courtesies

hello	*hola*	I speak a little Spanish	*hablo un poco de español*
good morning	*buenos días*	I don't speak Spanish	*no hablo español*
good afternoon/ evening	*buenas tardes/ noches*	do you speak English?	*¿hablas inglés?*
goodbye	*adiós/hasta luego*	I don't understand	*no entiendo*
pleased to meet you	*encantado/a*	please speak slowly	*habla despacio por favor*
how are you?	*¿cómo estás?*	I am very sorry	*lo siento mucho/ discúlpame*
I'm called ...	*me llamo ...*		
what is your name?	*¿cómo te llamas?*		
I'm fine, thanks	*muy bien, gracias*	what do you want?	*¿qué quieres?*
yes/no	*sí/no*	I want/would like	*quiero/quería*
please	*por favor*	I don't want it	*no lo quiero*
thank you (very much)	*(muchas) gracias*	good/bad	*bueno/malo*

Basic questions and requests

have you got a room for two people?	*¿tienes una habitación para dos personas?*	when does the bus leave (arrive)?	*¿a qué hora sale (llega) el autobús?*
how do I get to_?	*¿cómo llego a_?*	when?	*¿cuándo?*
how much does it cost?	*¿cuánto cuesta? ¿cuánto es?*	where is_?	*¿dónde está_?*
		where can I buy?	*¿dónde puedo comprar...?*
is VAT included?	*¿el IVA está incluido?*	where is the nearest petrol station?	*¿dónde está la gasolinera más cercana*
why?	*¿por qué?*		

Basic words and phrases

bank	*el banco*	cash	*efectivo*
bathroom/toilet	*el baño*	cheap	*barato/a*
to be	*ser, estar*	credit card	*la tarjeta de crédito*
bill	*la factura/ la cuenta*	exchange rate	*el tipo de cambio*

expensive	*caro/a*	public telephone	*el teléfono público*
to go	*ir*	shop	*la tienda*
to have	*tener, haber*	supermarket	*el supermercado*
market	*el mercado*	there is/are	*hay*
note/coin	*el billete/ la moneda*	there isn't/aren't	*no hay*
police (policeman)	*la policía (el policía)*	ticket office	*la taquilla*
		traveller's cheques	*los cheques de viaje*
post office	*el correo*		

Getting around

aeroplane	*el avión*	insured person	*el asegurado/ la asegurada*
airport	*el aeropuerto*		
arrival/departure	*la llegada/salida*	luggage	*el equipaje*
avenue	*la avenida*	motorway, freeway	*el autopista/ autovía*
border	*la frontera*		
bus station	*la estación de autobuses*	north/south/ west/east	*el norte, el sur, el oeste, el este*
bus	*el bus/ el autobús/ el camión*	oil	*el aceite*
		to park	*aparcar*
corner	*la esquina*	passport	*el pasaporte*
customs	*la aduana*	petrol/gasoline	*la gasolina*
left/right	*izquierda/ derecha*	puncture	*el pinchazo*
		street	*la calle*
ticket	*el billete*	that way	*por allí*
empty/full	*vacío/lleno*	this way	*por aquí*
highway, main road	*la carretera*	tyre	*el neumático*
insurance	*el seguro*	unleaded	*sin plomo*
		waiting room	*la sala de espera*
		to walk	*caminar/andar*

Accommodation

air conditioning	*el aire acondicionado*	restaurant	*el restaurante*
all-inclusive	*todo incluido*	room/bedroom	*el cuarto/ la habitación*
bathroom, private	*el baño privado*	sheets	*las sábanas*
bed, double/single	*la cama matrimonial/ sencilla*	shower	*la ducha*
		soap	*el jabón*
		toilet	*el inodoro*
blankets	*lasmantas*	toilet paper	*el papel higiénico*
to clean	*limpiar*	towels, clean/dirty	*las toallas limpias/sucias*
dining room	*el comedor*		
hotel	*el hotel*	water, hot/cold	*el agua caliente/ fría*
noisy	*ruidoso*		
pillow	*la almohada*		

Health

aspirin	*la aspirina*	diarrhoea	*la diarrea*
blood	*la sangre*	doctor	*el médico*
chemist	*la farmacia*	fever/sweat	*la fiebre/el sudor*
condoms	*los preservativos,*	pain	*el dolor*
	los condones	head	*la cabeza*
contact lenses	*los lentes de contacto*	period/sanitary towels	*la regla/*
contraceptives	*los anticonceptivos*		*las toallas*
contraceptive pill	*la píldora*		*femininas*
	anticonceptiva	stomach	*el estómago*

Family

family	*la familia*	boyfriend/girlfriend	*el novio/la novia*
brother/sister	*el hermano/*	friend	*el amigo/*
	la hermana		*la amiga*
daughter/son	*la hija/el hijo*	married	*casado/a*
father/mother	*el padre/lamadre*	single/unmarried	*soltero/a*
husband/wife	*el esposo (marido)/*		
	la mujer		

Months, days and time

January	*enero*	Friday	*viernes*
February	*febrero*	Saturday	*sábado*
March	*marzo*	Sunday	domingo
April	*abril*		
May	*mayo*	at one o'clock	*a launa*
June	*junio*	at half past two	*a las dos y media*
July	*julio*	at a quarter to three	*a las tres menos*
August	*agosto*		*cuarto*
September	*septiembre*	it's one o'clock	*es la una*
October	*octubre*	it's seven o'clock	*son las siete*
November	*noviembre*	it's six twenty	*son las seis y*
December	*diciembre*		*veinte*
		it's five to nine	*son las nueve*
Monday	*lunes*		*menos cinco*
Tuesday	*martes*	in ten minutes	*en diez minutos*
Wednesday	*miércoles*	five hours	*cinco horas*
Thursday	*jueves*	does it take long?	*¿tarda mucho?*

Numbers

one	*uno*	sixteen	*dieciséis*
two	*dos*	seventeen	*diecisiete*
three	*tres*	eighteen	*dieciocho*
four	*cuatro*	nineteen	*diecinueve*
five	*cinco*	twenty	*veinte*
six	*seis*	twenty-one	*veintiuno*
seven	*siete*	thirty	*treinta*
eight	*ocho*	forty	*cuarenta*
nine	*nueve*	fifty	*cincuenta*
ten	*diez*	sixty	*sesenta*
eleven	*once*	seventy	*setenta*
twelve	*doce*	eighty	*ochenta*
thirteen	*trece*	ninety	*noventa*
fourteen	*catorce*	hundred	*cien/ciento*
fifteen	*quince*	thousand	*mil*

Food glossary

It is impossible to be definitive about terms used. Different regions have numerous variants.

agua water
ahumado smoked
ajo garlic; *ajillo* means cooked in garlic, most commonly *gambas* or *pollo*
albóndigas meatballs
alcaparras capers
almejas small clams
alubias beans
anchoa preserved anchovy
atun tuna
bacalao salted cod
berenjena aubergine/eggplant
bistek steak
boquerones fresh anchovies
caballa mackerel
cabrito young goat, usually roasted
calamares squid
caldereta a stew of meat or fish
caldo a thin soup
callo tripe
carne meat
cazuela a stew, often of fish or seafood
cerdo pork
chipirones small squid
choco cuttlefish
chorizo a cured red sausage
chuleta/chuletilla chop
chuletón a massive T-bone steak
churro a fried dough-stick usually eaten with hot chocolate (*chocolate con churros*)
cigala giant prawn
cochinillo/lechón/tostón suckling pig
cocido a heavy stew, usually of meat and chickpeas/beans; sopa de cocido is the broth
cordero lamb

embutido any salami-type sausage
empanada a savoury pie
gambas prawns
higado liver
jamón ham
leche milk
lechuga lettuce
lenguado sole
lentejas lentils
lomo loin, usually sliced pork
lubina sea bass
Manchego Spain's national cheese made from ewe's milk
mantequilla butter
manzana apple
marisco shellfish
mejillones mussels
menudo tripe stew
merluza hake
mero grouper
miel honey
morcilla blood sausage
navajas razor-shells
ostra oyster
parrilla a mixed grill
pato duck
pechuga breast (usually chicken)
percebes goose-neck barnacles
pescado fish
pimientos peppers
pintxo/pincho bartop snack
pipas sunflower seeds, a common snack
pollo chicken
pulpo octopus
queso cheese
rape monkfish

relleno/a stuffed
revuelto scrambled eggs
riñones kidneys
salchichón a salami-like sausage
salmorejo a thicker version of gazpacho

salpicón a seafood salad
secreto a cut of pork loin
sepia cuttlefish
setas wild mushrooms, often superb
solomillo beef fillet steak
zanahoria carrot

Index → Entries in **bold** refer to maps

FOOTPRINT

Features

Credits

Footprint credits

Editor: Nicola Gibbs
Production and layout: Emma Bryers
Maps: Kevin Feeney
Colour section: Angus Dawson

Publisher: Patrick Dawson
Managing Editor: Felicity Laughton
Administration: Elizabeth Taylor
Advertising sales and marketing:
John Sadler, Kirsty Holmes,
Debbie Wylde

Photography credits
Front cover: Philip Lange/
Shutterstock.com
Back cover: Top: 135pixels/
Shutterstock.com.
Bottom: Madrugada Verde/
Shutterstock.com

Colour section
Inside front cover: Tupungato/
Shutterstock.com, thegiffary/
Shutterstock.com, Filimonov/
Shutterstock.com.
Page 1: holbox/Shutterstock.com.
Page 2: Travel Library Limited/
Superstock. **Page 4**: Christian Kober/
Superstock, LOOK-foto/Superstock.
Page 5: holbox/Shutterstock.
com, Olaf Speier/Shutterstock.com,
Christian Bertrand/Dreamstime.com.
Page 7: José Fuste Raga/Superstock,
Michael Kolvenbach/Superstock,
Antonio Real/Superstock, Iakov
Filimonov/Shutterstock.com,
holbox/Shutterstock.com. **Page 8**:
Davyria MC/Shutterstock.com.

Printed in Spain by GraphyCems

Publishing information
Footprint Valencia & Costa Blanca
2nd edition
© Footprint Handbooks Ltd
July 2015

ISBN: 978 1 910120 49 1
CIP DATA: A catalogue record for this
book is available from the British Library

® Footprint Handbooks and the
Footprint mark are a registered
trademark of Footprint Handbooks Ltd

Published by Footprint
6 Riverside Court
Lower Bristol Road
Bath BA2 3DZ, UK
T +44 (0)1225 469141
F +44 (0)1225 469461
footprinttravelguides.com

Distributed in the USA by
National Book Network, Inc.

Every effort has been made to ensure
that the facts in this guidebook are
accurate. However, travellers should still
obtain advice from consulates, airlines,
etc, about travel and visa requirements
before travelling. The authors and
publishers cannot accept responsibility
for any loss, injury or inconvenience
however caused.